DOING BUSINESS IN AFRICA

CONNECTING CAPITAL TO AFRICAN OPPORTUNITIES

Dr Rufaro Nyakatawa
(Mucheka), PhD

DOING BUSINESS IN AFRICA
Connecting Capital to African Opportunities

Copyright © 2023 Dr Rufaro Nyakatawa

All rights reserved. This book or any portion thereof may not be reproduced or used in any manner whatsoever without the express written permission of the publisher except for the use of brief quotations in a book review or scholarly journal.

First Printing: 2023

ISBN
978-0-6397-8910-1

Tahera Mucheka: Creative Editor

Printed and Bound in South Africa by PRINT ON DEMAND
Typeset and Cover Design by Wade Hunkin

The author may be contacted at: Rufaro.Nyakatawa@rdkcapital.com

ABOUT THE AUTHOR

Dr Rufaro Nyakatawa (formerly Mucheka) is a seasoned Management Consultant with more than 20 years' experience travelling and working across Africa. As the Founder and CEO of the business consultancy, RDK Capital, Dr Rufaro advises businesses on how to successfully enter, set up and conduct business in different African countries. She is supported by an experienced team of associates across the continent in markets such as South Africa, Rwanda, Ghana, Nigeria, Tanzania, Zambia, Namibia, Lesotho and Zimbabwe.

Having been raised in the poor rural setting of Nyanga, Zimbabwe, Dr Rufaro is passionate about economic development in Africa and the financial inclusion of women. She finds inspiration in Mahatma Gandhi's exhortation to, 'Be the change you want to see in the world'.

Dr Rufaro has a Doctor of Philosophy (PhD) and Masters in Business Administration (MBA) from the University of Cape Town, and is a Certified Financial Planner (CFP®) and a Trust and Estate Practitioner (TEP) professional. As a Non-Executive Director on several commercial boards, Dr Rufaro is known for providing pragmatic advice. She also serves on volunteer boards, including the Cherie Blair Foundation and Women in Tech (a global movement). Dr Rufaro is a renowned international speaker and thought leader, who is a mentor and connector of people to people and opportunities.

Dr Rufaro spent five years in key markets across Africa helping a large corporate to successfully set up a sustainable wealth management business. The vast experience she acquired in the different countries inspired her to pursue a PhD on Doing Business in Africa. This book is based on the experiential learnings Dr Rufaro acquired during her journey, as well as her current experiences as a Management Consultant helping clients explore opportunities on the continent. Her extensive experience led her to become an authority on this subject, given her decades of experience in business strategy, managing strategic projects, business development and business planning. This experience and her philosophy of Connecting Capital to African Opportunities have led her to share her invaluable knowledge through this book.

PREFACE

I was born and raised in the rural area of Nyanga, Zimbabwe, where I had a very limited window into the developed world. My imagination about what the universe outside my small community might look like, ran wild. This inventive picture of what the world could be inspired my life journey.

I was fortunate to go to schools where my imagination was nurtured; education became the vehicle I used to explore the world beyond my limited horizon. It was the tradition in my hometown to send children who did well to boarding schools for their secondary education. As a result, I was sent to a girls boarding school, Monte Cassino, located far from my home, which meant that I travelled even further than the town in which my father lived and worked. During my first four years at boarding school, my horizons expanded; I learnt new things and came to a better understanding of how the world worked. For A levels, I went to another girls boarding school, St David's High Bonda, which was a larger school and had a reputation for academic excellence. My passion for knowledge was nurtured by meeting fellow students from different areas and backgrounds, stopping over in the small town my father lived in, and ultimately, going to university in Harare, the capital city of Zimbabwe.

By watching television and taking part in high school trips, my imagination was sparked even further about life beyond my immediate environment. I developed a keen interest in travel, so when I started working, I enjoyed my newfound freedom by travelling to new towns or points of interest with friends, including going to South Africa on shopping excursions. A fire was ignited in me – I wanted to know and experience more! Coming from a background of having nothing, being *anywhere* else intrigued me. An opportunity to work in Bophuthatswana, then a homeland of South Africa, presented itself a year after my university graduation. I could not say, 'No'!

As my career progressed, my curiosity about the two fields I was most passionate about – education and travel – continued to grow. At that point, South Africa became home. To expand my knowledge, I completed a Diploma in Project Management, which I followed up with a Master's Degree in Business Administration and a Postgraduate Diploma in in Financial Planning, now a Certified Financial Planner (CFP). Between my studies, I explored other cities in neighbouring countries. As a family, we regularly explored other Southern African and international countries. It quickly became clear that South African companies dominated the landscapes of neighbouring countries; the low psychic distance meant that we could get most South African products anywhere in the region. On these travels, I became fascinated with how businesses were set up differently in other countries. As an example, I was intrigued by how you could get anything and everything from informal markets in certain African markets. My interest was heightened in 2013, when I travelled to Nigeria for the first time. Having been based in South Africa for over 20 years by that point, it was fascinating to see how many South African businesses had set up shop in Africa's largest economy. Given that

I had seen some of these companies in some shape or form in other African countries I had travelled to, it was clear to me that companies were discovering huge opportunities doing business in other African markets. As the Head of Business Strategy for a financial advisory business, strategy was central to how my brain was wired and was the filter for all my thought processes. The two key questions I pondered were:
- Why do some companies succeed when they expand into other African countries, yet others fail?
- For those that succeed, what strategies do they use?

Wanting to find the answers to these questions further fuelled my interest in exploring the continent. I realised that we, as Africans, cannot just sit back and expect others to come and build the continent for us. Instead of complaining about our problems and the things that do not work, entrepreneurs and problem solvers can play a key role in changing the narrative about Africa. As Africans, we understand the problems that affect us better than anyone else. In some cases, we have ingenious ideas on how to solve them. I wanted to be the change I wanted to see in the world, but where should I begin?

I soon realised that I would have to use *what I had* to make a change to *where I was*. As what I had was relatively limited, I decided to sharpen my saw with knowledge. My passion for making a change in Africa became a calling, which led to me expanding my knowledge of wealth management and business strategy... *what I had*. Yet despite this knowledge, I knew that I lacked a complete understanding of how to do business in Africa. For me to make a meaningful contribution on the continent, I realised that it was critical for me to understand and experience first-hand how business is done in other African countries.

While I wanted to pursue the 'learning by doing' approach to better understand the African context, I also knew that I was a latecomer to the sector and that academics would accelerate my growth. At that time, I was Head of Strategy for Nedbank Financial Planning, a business within one of the big four banks in South Africa. Simultaneously, I pursued a PhD in Commerce so that I could acquire further expertise, specifically in business management. To put my plan into action, I decided on a dissertation topic, looked for a supervisor and registered with the University of Cape Town for the 2014 intake. My dissertation, which focused on doing business in Africa, was titled, *An exploration of strategies used by South African companies to expand into other African markets.*

In light of my desire to learn by doing, I also jumped at an opportunity where I could use my expertise in financial planning to add value to a partner of Nedbank's, Ecobank, which had a footprint in 34 countries in Africa. My role was to support them with the creation and set-up of a wealth management business, and despite having to jump through many hoops (as is usually the case with any uncommon initiative), the business case was approved in 2016. That year I became the lead for this strategic partnership initiative – my internationalisation journey had begun!

I increasingly gained experiential learning whilst spending time in different African countries and studying remotely. By dividing my focus between theory and practice, I could implement an internationalisation strategy for my employer, while studying the strategies implemented by other South African companies as they expanded into Africa. When I graduated with my with my PhD in 2019, my academic journey had been translated into a practical toolkit built upon experiential learning. Since I had visited many African countries over the years and been introduced to doing business outside South Africa with my first trip to Namibia in 2015, I had accumulated extensive local knowledge and experiences in different countries on the continent. Since then, I have continued to garner invaluable practical knowledge that is pertinent to business leaders who are considering Africa as a frontier market, international businesses wanting to expand their operations into Africa or other African countries, and those wanting relevant insights regarding what strategies to use when entering markets of interest on the continent.

> *For me to make a meaningful contribution on the continent, I realised that it was critical for me to understand and experience first-hand how business is done in other African countries."*

CONTENTS

	ABOUT THE AUTHOR		ii
	PREFACE		iv
	ACRONYMS		1
ONE	**INTRODUCTION**		2
TWO	**INTERNATIONALISATION OF BUSINESSES**		6
	2.1	**THEORIES**	6
	2.1.1	THE RESOURCE-BASED VIEW	7
	2.1.2	ECLECTIC PARADIGM	8
	2.1.3	THE UPPSALA MODEL	9
	2.2	**FACTORS INFLUENCING INTERNATIONALISATION STRATEGY PROCESSES**	10
	2.2.1	PSYCHIC DISTANCE	11
	2.2.2	COMPANY RESOURCES	15
	2.2.3	STRATEGIC CHOICE	19
	2.2.4	STRATEGIC CHOICES FOR AFRICA	21
	2.3	**DOING BUSINESS IN AFRICA**	24
	2.3.1	WHY IS AFRICA AN ATTRACTIVE MARKET FOR BUSINESS EXPANSION?	27
	2.3.2	BUSINESS MODELS USED TO EXPAND OPERATIONS ACROSS THE AFRICAN CONTINENT	31
THREE	**MARKET RESEARCH**		34
	3.1	**SURVEY OF COMPANIES DOING BUSINESS IN MULTIPLE AFRICAN COUNTRIES**	35

	3.1.1	INTRODUCTION	**35**
	3.1.2	MARKET CHOICE	**36**
	3.1.3	SURVEY RESULTS AND FINDINGS	**36**
	3.2	**CASE STUDIES OF INTERNATIONALISING COMPANIES**	**56**
	3.2.1	INTRODUCTION	**56**
	3.2.2	THE PARTNERSHIP-BASED INTERNATIONALISATION MODEL	**57**
	3.2.3	THE OWNERSHIP-BASED INTERNATIONALISATION MODEL	**58**
	3.2.4	COMPARATIVE ANALYSIS OF OWNERSHIP-BASED VS. PARTNERSHIP-BASED MODELS	**60**
	3.2.5	SUMMARY OF RESULTS: COMPARING THE TWO COMPANIES	**93**
	3.2.6	HOW DID THESE COMPANIES CONQUER AFRICA?	**96**
FOUR	**WHAT WORKS IN AFRICA**		**100**
	4.1	**SUCCESSFUL EXPANSION OF BUSINESSES INTO MULTIPLE AFRICAN COUNTRIES**	**100**
	4.1.1	THE TOOLKIT	**101**
	4.1.2	THE PROCESSES	**104**
	4.2	**LIVED EXPERIENCES FROM LOCALS AND MY PERSONAL EXPERIENCE**	**105**
	4.2.1	EASE OF DOING BUSINESS	**107**
	4.2.2	RWANDA	**109**
	4.2.3	ZAMBIA	**111**
	4.2.4	GHANA	**113**
	4.2.5	NIGERIA	**114**
	4.2.6	TANZANIA	**117**
	4.2.7	DEMOCRATIC REPUBLIC OF CONGO (DRC)	**119**
FIVE	**FINAL INSIGHTS**		**122**
SIX	**CONCLUSION**		**128**
SEVEN	**REFERENCES**		**134**

ACRONYMS	
AfCFTA	African Continental Free Trade Area
CEO	Chief Executive Officer
COMESA	Common Market for Eastern and Southern Africa
ECOWAS	Economic Community of West African States
EMNE	Emerging Multinational Enterprise
FDI	Foreign Direct Investment
CSA	Company Specific Advantage
FTA	Free Trade Agreement
GDP	Gross Domestic Product
HR	Human Resources
JSE	Johannesburg Stock Exchange
MNE	Multinational Enterprise
OLI	Ownership, Location and Internationalisation
SADC	Southern African Development Community
RBV	Resource-based View

ONE

INTRODUCTION

Organisations, individuals and the media often describe Africa as being beset with problems, yet people with an entrepreneurial mindset, a good business sense and a knack for innovation realise that problems can also present opportunities. These opportunities include solving some of the world's most complex challenges and breaking down barriers. It is important to remember that Africa is not one homogenous entity but rather 54 independent countries, each with its own jurisdictional independence and nuances. Africa's economic and cultural typographies provide fertile ground for growth and innovation, especially for companies seeking opportunities to advance their global competitiveness outside their national borders.

The African Continental Free Trade Area (AfCFTA) has brought hope for regional trade integration that would stimulate economic activity and increase development on the continent. While the goal of free continental trade is yet to be realised, work is underway to build on the foundation set by the various regional trade blocs. For decades, the Economic Community of West African States (ECOWAS), the Common Market for Eastern and Southern Africa (COMESA) and the Southern African Development Community (SADC) have been working together to promote economic growth and industrialisation through infrastructure, investment and the development of new industries. The African Continental Free Trade Area (AfCFTA) is viewed as a welcome socio-economic objective and represents an important milestone in the context of the Pan African imperative of achieving an economically integrated Africa.

This focus on integration could shed some light on China and India's engagement with Africa. While other nations are looking east to India & China for Foreign Direct Investment (FDI) opportunities, these countries in the east have clear African strategies. China is intent on promoting its peaceful expansion to become a global powerhouse, with its government playing a key role in propelling its local 'dragons' to internationalise. These 'dragons' are Chinese companies that have the appetite and potential to do well outside China. The government has created institutions that facilitate internationalisation, and primarily control and coordinate the business activities of Chinese enterprises in host countries.[1] India, on the other hand, has opted for a more pragmatic economic approach in its quest for rapid industrial growth aligned with its global aspirations. This approach has largely taken the form of takeovers, such as Bharti Airtel's purchase of Zain Africa in 2008. More recent statistics compiled by the Reserve Bank of India shows that Indian companies invested a cumulative total of USD 13.8 billion between 2015 and 2019 in African countries.[2]

Like their Asian counterparts, South African companies have also set their sights on doing business across the continent. Indeed, despite the uneven institutional landscape presented by many African countries, some large South African corporates, including MTN, Shoprite and SAB Miller, have successfully set up numerous sustainable operations outside their home country. This is exciting as it proves that home-grown African companies can successfully navigate business opportunities on the continent. Yet despite these notable successes, some South African businesses have failed dismally in their internationalisation strategies. It is thus essential to investigate why some companies succeed in their growth strategies, while others do not.

Limited research has been conducted on how African companies deal with issues such as psychic distance, company resources and strategic choice in their internationalisation strategies. My intention with this book is to explore these economic and social factors involved in setting up a business in Africa, focusing on the private sector. As a result, I do not delve into each country's economic policies, but rather provide a general overview of how certain important factors influence the planning and implementation processes for companies internationalising on the continent. For multinational companies that have a footprint in some African countries but have reached an inflection point and are battling to grow, my second objective is to offer other lenses through which to view the market conditions. Finally, I aspire to create awareness of how business is done in Africa so that those with great ideas can be tactical, giving their business the best possible chance of success from the outset. This will ultimately create employment, build wealth and help develop sustainable communities.

> *I aspire to create awareness of how business is done in Africa so that those with great ideas can be tactical, giving their business the best possible chance of success from the outset."*

TWO

INTERNATIONALISATION OF BUSINESSES

2.1 THEORIES

Before you decide to put down roots, picking the right location is vital. Issues that businesses must consider include geographic location, level of economic activity, availability of transportation, size of population and trade barriers. After all, companies are in the business of making money and must, therefore, choose locations that will maximise their profits.[3] Doing business outside one's national borders requires decision-makers to have specific knowledge before they commit resources to an identified market. Although companies have unique strategies for determining their ideal locations, literature shows that they also establish themselves internationally in a staged manner, initially targeting culturally, geographically and economically similar host countries. In addition, they use markers, such as population, profitability and international experience, to help establish their level of comfort with a new venture.[4]

It is important to understand one or more relevant internationalisation theories if one is to gain a complete picture of the various aspects of growing across borders. Although new markets present opportunities, they also pose challenges. These include destination governments protecting their local businesses by imposing trade tariffs, misinterpretation of laws, language barriers and distinct business practices. The uneven economic terrain of international locations makes it difficult to apply just one theoretical framework, so a deep understanding and thorough application of several is typically necessary.

As I'm sure you know, there is no one-size-fits-all solution to doing business in Africa; each of the 54 countries on the continent present unique nuances and opportunities. But enough talk... let's get to understanding the key models.

2.1.1 THE RESOURCE-BASED VIEW

The resource-based view (RBV) of a company is grounded in the assumption that a company can deliver a sustainable competitive advantage when its resources are managed effectively. The RBV believes in the collection of valuable tangible or intangible resources at a company's disposal, which offers the company a unique advantage.[5] Company resources include knowledge, capabilities, attributes and the organisational processes that enable it to improve and become more effective.[6] Intuitively, it makes sense to view a company's strengths based on what it is capable of. A company that is in constant pursuit of the renewal, reconfiguration and re-creation of its resources, capabilities and core competencies can enhance its competitiveness by remaining up to date with current information and processes.

Organisations that operate in developed countries benefit from mature institutional environments that provide supporting resources, e.g., the company does not have to invest in developing good roads for transportation. Because these supporting resources are external to the company and it cannot transfer them abroad, when such a company expands to a less developed country, it is deprived of these resources. Conversely, for companies from developing nations where the home environment does not provide such supporting resources, the company either develops them itself or learns how to operate in their absence. Understanding the varying resources of the company and its market environment enhances its strategy and ensures minimum wastage.

2.1.2 ECLECTIC PARADIGM

The eclectic paradigm, also referred to as the OLI (ownership, location and internationalisation) framework, is a three-tiered evaluation framework. Companies can use it to determine how to look at a foreign market opportunity and decide whether it is a good investment option. Ownership refers to a company's specific competencies and an understanding of how these develop; location refers to the transferability of a company's competencies between markets; and internationalisation describes the various modes of market entry in a competitive context.

Figure 1: An example of how to use the OLI Model

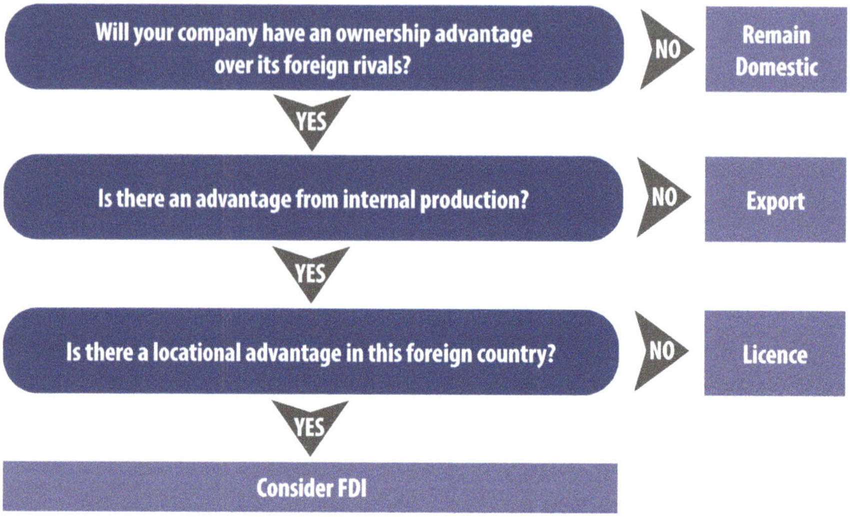

```
Will your company have an ownership advantage
over its foreign rivals?  --NO--> Remain Domestic
        |
       YES
        |
Is there an advantage from internal production?  --NO--> Export
        |
       YES
        |
Is there a locational advantage in this foreign country?  --NO--> Licence
        |
       YES
        |
    Consider FDI
```

An organisation's choice of location is influenced by a combination of company-specific advantages (CSAs) and country-specific factors, such as the availability of natural resources, access to markets and assets that complement the CSAs. The decision for a company that operates in a certain industry to enter a specific host country depends on the motives of the enterprise. For example, the parameters influencing an American multinational to invest in a copper mine in Zambia are unlikely to be similar to those influencing an investment by a South African construction management company in Senegal. Companies internationalise because they identify advantages in transferring some moveable resources (such as knowledge, intermediate products, etc.) across a national border to be combined with an immobile, or less mobile, resource or opportunity.[7]

Although opportunities appear to be abundant depending on the choice of market, conducting transactions in a foreign country has certain disadvantages, especially when a foreign company is pitted against indigenous companies. These include government-instituted barriers to trade and an incomplete understanding of laws, languages and business practices.

2.1.3 THE UPPSALA MODEL

The Uppsala Model focuses on the evolution process of the multinational enterprise. The first step is to commit resources, after which it is all about developing processes through learning. This phased development of company internationalisation is described as an incremental, risk-averse and reluctant adjustment to changes in a company or its environment. Related to this approach is the sequential nature of 'learning and doing' during internationalisation, where organisations pursuing this strategy start from nearby markets before moving to environments that are further afield and unfamiliar.

This model is consistent with the dynamic capabilities view, in the sense that when new knowledge is learnt or created, highlights the need for ongoing learning. This, in turn lead to the creation of new business models. The more business leaders understand the foundations of business success in different African countries, the higher the likelihood that they will become more committed to their internationalisation strategy and innovate to make it work in their chosen markets. Companies find methods of bridging perceived differences by acquiring country-specific knowledge and hiring executives with prior knowledge of the dynamics in the chosen market.

The Uppsala Model highlights three types of dynamic capabilities considered to be of special importance for international development:

- The opportunity development capability is the ability to identify opportunities and mobilise relevant resources.
- The internationalisation capability is the ability to approach and develop different markets and locations under various circumstances.
- The networking capability encompasses the ability to build, sustain and coordinate relationships in a network-type context.

2.2 FACTORS INFLUENCING INTERNATIONALISATION STRATEGY PROCESSES

'Strategy' is a way of thinking about a business – assessing its strengths, diagnosing its weaknesses and envisioning its possibilities. It is a continuous evolutionary process, rather than an outcome or endpoint. Strategy development, therefore, requires companies to consider both the present and the future in order to be able to identify and bridge a gap and to make the organisation competitive over the long-term.[9] The ability to discover and take advantage of business opportunities in multiple countries is no longer reserved for large, mature corporations. Given the availability of low-cost communication technology and high-speed transportation, it has made international markets accessible to both small and emerging entrepreneurs.[10] Psychic and cultural distances with a destination country are important considerations; the smaller the cultural distance, the easier it is for multinational companies to operate with a fair understanding of the cultural norms and beliefs of the local market. A standard strategy cannot work across different countries, however; multinational companies that try to apply a 'one-size-fits-all' model in developing markets struggle to make this work.

2.2.1 PSYCHIC DISTANCE

When a company expands outside its national borders, it faces a different set of conditions in the host country to those it is familiar with at home. Some of these factors include differences in language, education, business practices, cultures, institutions and industrial development. As such, psychic distance is a fundamental consideration in internationalisation decision-making as it can create either an advantage or a disadvantage for companies. Generally, views on psychic distance are subjective and can lead to the 'distance paradox' *(Figure 2)*. This paradox describes a phenomenon where the apparent proximity between a home country and an internationalisation target may inadvertently lead managers to overlook important differences.[11]

Another key issue when looking at different markets is that of economic distance. Indices such as wealth and per capita income in a host country are key characteristics that highlight the economic distance between countries, which can be used to determine the potential economic benefit of doing business in a new market.[12]

Figure 2: An illustration of the distance paradox

The decision on where and when to internationalise aims to maximise a company's ability to realise its full potential in a foreign country. This is why many companies rely on signals of similarity and dissimilarity. Similarity comparisons are a useful mental tool through which humans make sense of the world. These include drawing inferences and interpretations, understanding new concepts more fully, developing courses of action to pursue and, ultimately, making decisions. This creates a foundation for identifying commonalities and provides the perceived safety of 'sameness'.[13] Most markets have their own sets of key consumers, competitors and owners of factors of production – collectively known as the main actors. If a new company does not know who the main actors are, it has the liability of 'outsidership'.[14]

CULTURE

The more commonalities there are between the home and potential destination country, the more likely that country will be selected, as leaders tend to enter markets that are similar to their own in terms of language, business systems, norms and level of economic development. Multinationals that enter small developing markets close to their home countries also have a greater chance of success, as such markets typically rely heavily on products or services from larger, more developed markets.[15] Another successful way to integrate a company's culture, systems and competencies is through the use of diaspora members, i.e., people who do not live in their home countries but rather live and work abroad.[16] These people are highly treasured resources for EMNEs in particular, because they originate from the targeted markets. A key aspect about people in a diaspora is that they are typically better off than people in their countries of origin in terms of tertiary education, income, technical skills, wealth, global consciousness and network connectivity.[17] These individuals, when placed in management positions in their countries of birth, reduce the cultural distance and make it easier for the EMNE to do business. Most multinational organisations would prefer not to change their business models as they expand into other markets, yet for organisations to succeed, they need to be adaptable and accommodate local cultures, both in their human resources practices and overall strategies.[18]

GEOGRAPHY

Geographic location can be a key factor in the success or failure of a company. In particular, geographic complexities can affect operational efficiency and should thus be thoroughly assessed before companies expand into new territories.[19] With varying institutional landscapes, emerging market economies are not homogeneous, even if they are in the same geographic region.[20] This can be compounded by colonial history, especially in Africa, where neighbouring countries' psychic distances can be significant because of boundaries imposed by colonialists. A common language can be used to mitigate psychic distance and facilitate cross-border internationalisation into neighbouring countries, however. In Africa, communities in the vicinity of a border generally speak similar languages, making it easier for internationalisation. For South African businesses, as English is the main business language, they are better able to internationalise in English-speaking countries.[21] The same can be said for companies from French-speaking countries being better able to internationalise into other Francophone countries.

INSTITUTIONS

Institutions play a key role in lessening uncertainty and creating stable market conditions to facilitate business transactions and growth while reducing information costs. An absence of institutions such as intermediaries, regulatory systems and contract-enforcing mechanisms thus makes it difficult for companies to do business. As not every institutional void can be rectified by governments, the private sector can create and own intermediaries that facilitate the flow of information in the market between private companies and governments. Some multinational enterprises from developing countries improve their internationalisation strategies by exploiting their knowledge of certain market segments, having learnt to play the role of market institutions.[6] In other words, they have found that addressing institutional voids creates value. Accenture[22] gave some examples of South African companies that have created institutions in certain African countries to facilitate their business, i.e.,:

- SABMiller repaired roads that linked its processing plants to its customers;
- MultiChoice builds its local capabilities by training local staff; and
- collaboration between Massmart and Shoprite helps the two companies minimise their infrastructure costs.

In these ways, we can see that an organisation's strategies can negatively or positively influence institutions.

2.2.2 COMPANY RESOURCES

Important resources that should not be underestimated are core competencies, i.e., skills that integrate multiple streams of knowledge and technology and are vital for an organisation's overall success, as they assist in building competitive 'moats'. Competitive advantages arise from developing and deploying unique, valuable, inimitable and non-substitutable resources. Companies operating in developed countries benefit from a mature institutional environment that provides supporting resources that are not transferable. Conversely, companies from developing nations may not enjoy such supporting resources and will therefore either develop them themselves or learn how to operate without them. The latter can be a benefit, as companies from countries with less developed environments can transfer the knowledge generated from operating in such conditions with limited infrastructure[23] to new host countries during internationalisation.

KNOWLEDGE, LEARNING AND CREATION

Most customers in emerging markets are at the 'bottom of the pyramid', so the affordability of products and solutions is critical.[24] Simple aspects of customisation, such as packaging, can create a competitive edge in local markets, as local winners package products innovatively to make them affordable[25], convenient to use and easy to store. This also minimises waste as people only use what they need. In South Africa, when Old Mutual, an insurance company, saw a gap in the mutual funds and long-term investments business at the bottom of the pyramid, it closed the gap by creating solutions such as a low-cost transactional account. In the process, it became a market leader in this field. The company has also found new ways of creating innovation in its home operation, using lessons learnt from some of its other African operations.[26]

LEADERSHIP

Effective leadership engenders a sense of belonging and encourages employees to go above and beyond for their employer. Charismatic leadership, supported by knowledge and a solid team, is a useful formula for effectively leading a company as it enters new markets.[27] The lenses through which business problems and solutions are often identified and resolved reflect an executive's background and functional experience. The diversity of foreign markets, especially in emerging markets, threatens companies' strategies because of the variety of rivals, suppliers and buyers. Employing leaders who have prior learning associated with international experience should thus result in fewer mistakes and a higher likelihood of success.

INFLUENCE OF COMPANY RESOURCES ON PLANNING

Frameworks are valuable in ensuring that an organisation has not just a strategy, but a sound strategy.[28] This is vital, as a framework is a tool that can be used to logically analyse an issue and build a structured response. An example of a framework that can be considered by businesses expanding into other markets is an issue tree, which is used globally as a problem-solving framework by companies like

McKinsey. An issue tree *(see Figure 3)* can be described as a structured way of problem solving; it breaks a problem down into mutually exclusive and collectively exhaustive components.

Figure 3: An example of an issue tree to help determine how to increase market share

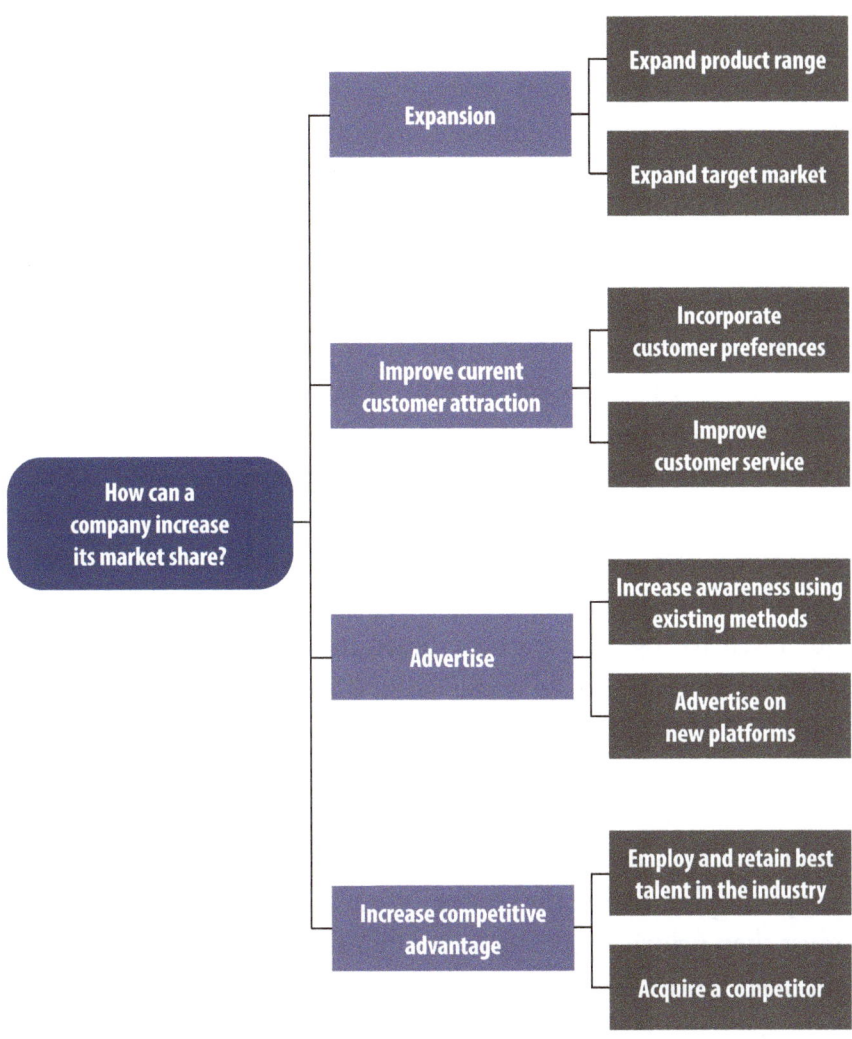

Although frameworks are important in strategy construction, it is an endless evolutionary process, not a be-all-and-end-all process. A good strategy provides a clear roadmap on the 'what' and the 'how', but a successful internationalisation strategy depends on a company's ability to modify its business model based on early learnings and adapt the model for entry into new markets. The leadership team therefore needs to have the aptitude and appetite to fine-tune the original strategy to make it relevant and work in the new market. In contrast, an example of a poor strategy is where a company fails to model how accessible its products and/or services will be to a wide selection of customers in emerging markets. This type of unsuccessful strategy fails to account for inadequate infrastructure and does not take into account the voice of the customer or potential problems with the supply chain. A successful business model includes a customer value proposition and profit formula, as well as the key processes and critical resources that the company must use to repeatedly deliver value.

INFLUENCE OF COMPANY RESOURCES ON IMPLEMENTATION

Successful strategies involve getting a product into the market quickly, learning from the experience, moving on to the next phase of development and, in some cases, being ahead of competitors with new ideas. The implementation of any strategy relies heavily on leadership; without key people orchestrating a product launch smoothly and effectively, the process will take much longer than originally planned. Buy-in and a good understanding among the people implementing the strategy are also essential.[29] The company must then prioritise setting ways of measuring progress to identify red flags before it is too late. New ventures will always be loaded with risks and some managers fall into the trap of focusing on one key risk at the expense of others because they do not use a risk management framework. The more risks that can be identified and eliminated, the higher the probability of success. It is critical to learn lessons from experience before putting a detailed plan into action.[30]

2.2.3 STRATEGIC CHOICE

Fitzhugh Dodson, an American clinical psychologist, once said, 'Without goals and plans to reach these, you are like a ship that has set sail with no destination'. You must have a strategy on how you plan to win, which could entail obtaining a greater market share, successfully finding a suitable partner to merge with, or entering the African context. Two key factors must be considered before a business develops its strategy to enter any foreign market: motivation and mode of entry.[31] Motivation refers to 'why' the company has decided to enter a specific foreign market, e.g., whether it wants to exploit an advantage it has, strengthen an existing one or develop new capabilities. Mode of entry relates to 'how' to enter the chosen market, for example, through exporting, licensing, a joint venture or a sole proprietorship.

The size of a firm positively correlates with its entry mode. In other words, larger firms with more resources are able to absorb the initial cost of internationalisation and will opt for a higher degree of control, such as being wholly owned rather than developing partnerships. On the other hand, companies can protect their internal resources and capabilities from risks due to unfamiliarity by getting a partner that wields substantial capabilities to fill institutional voids.[32] Multinationals and emerging market-based companies that do not build full businesses to fill institutional voids face a set of strategic choices and a menu of options to respond to them *(Table 1)*.

Table 1: Various strategic choices businesses should consider[33]

STRATEGIC CHOICE	OPTIONS FOR MULTINATIONALS
REPLICATE OR ADAPT?	**REPLICATE** your existing business model and exploit your relative advantage of global brand, credibility, know-how, talent, finance and other factor inputs. **ADAPT** business models, products or organisations to institutional voids.
COMPETE ALONE OR COLLABORATE?	**COMPETE** alone. **COLLABORATE** by acquiring the necessary capabilities to navigate new territory through local partnerships or joint ventures.
ADAPT OR ATTEMPT TO CHANGE THE MARKET CONTEXT?	**ADAPT** to the market context. **CHANGE THE MARKET** context by filling the institutional voids through expanding service delivery.
ENTER, WAIT OR EXIT?	**ENTER** the market. **WAIT** in the market despite the challenges of institutional voids. **EXIT** and look for opportunities elsewhere.

International strategic decisions are multi-faceted, with leaders having to identify attractive markets, select appropriate entry modes, choose the timing of the entry, and consider product-service adaptations amongst diverse market choices and external environment conditions.[34]

2.2.4 STRATEGIC CHOICES FOR AFRICA
ENTRY MODE: PARTNERSHIP
Partnerships are typically selected to minimise a company's exposure to downside risk. This entry mode essentially offers lower levels of control and investment risk[35], thus relationships and customising solutions with a local partner are key. The chosen partner should be able to use its knowledge of customer preferences and local factors of production to help create a platform for success.[36] Further, it must have mechanisms in place to navigate emerging market nuances. Selecting an appropriate partner is a critical strategic factor to achieve the desired goal of overcoming institutional voids, so it must be done judiciously. Rather enter the market later than risk getting into bed with an unsuitable or possibly corrupt partner.

ENTRY MODE: OWNERSHIP
Some businesses prefer an ownership model as they make their debut into unknown territory; their confidence could be inspired by the success of their home business model. In the case of Standard Bank, one of the executives who participated in the case study interviews indicated that, "The market demands. If you look at just the local space, there is Lesotho, there is Eswatini, there is South Africa – not just one country. So it makes sense to be in at least two countries. Because of the movement of people between these three countries, you can't draw a line even though there are boundaries that serve these countries."

Businesses that prefer this model have a differentiated product, a track record and global customer affinity. As companies using the ownership model do not want to share their profits, they bear all the risks of being innovative, adaptable and relevant to their customers' changing needs, as well as staying ahead of their competition.[37] Multinational companies that prefer this model tend to use their acquired international experience and credibility to gain the trust of host countries.

TIMING: FIRST MOVER

Being the first provider in a market or industry allows you to set the stage for your company and brand, as you can build customer loyalty before any other competitor does. Companies that can manage this enjoy the benefits of being the first participants in new product markets, reputation effects, more stable sales volumes and pro-active domination of distribution and communication channels.[38] They are also able to learn the hard lessons sooner and to adapt their products accordingly. South African companies, such as MTN, Shoprite and Standard Bank, with their early experience of African business conditions and insight into African societies and markets, have an advantage when they act as a bridge into Africa and can realise value sooner than businesses from other parts of the world.[39]

TIMING: LATECOMER

Latecomers are already at a disadvantage when they enter new markets as they still need to learn about their potential host countries. The local regulatory landscape, competitors and what the consumer wants are issues that must be understood. Fortunately, it is not all bad news. In some cases, being a late mover allows a company to fill a gap that the early mover missed and to challenge the status quo. To avoid getting into trouble after forgetting they had homework, many children look for the smartest child in the class to ask for the answers. In the same way, latecomers tend to choose mergers and acquisitions (M&A) as the fastest way to enter markets and obtain required resources in a host country.[40] Through learning and discovery, the latecomer has a fighting chance in unfamiliar territory.

INFLUENCE OF STRATEGIC CHOICE ON PLANNING AND IMPLEMENTATION

In emerging markets, a key factor is sourcing reliable data. For this reason, institutions like Ernst & Young have developed toolsets like *Growing Beyond Borders*. Another helpful indicator is the World Bank's + *indicator*. These tools can help assist in making sense of Africa's data deficits and highlight opportunities across the continent. By using both qualitative and quantitative tools, executives can reach reasonable conclusions. Unfortunately, simply having the 'correct' information does not guarantee that a strategy will succeed. Some strategies fail because a competitor enters the market with the same, or a similar, idea before your company launches its idea into the market. Once an idea has missed the timing in the market, the essential window of opportunity is lost.[41]

It is unclear why, but there is a misconception that one can get away with shortcuts in developing countries. Put simply, when a company chooses not to follow standards, the world finds out. Excellent execution and good governance are thus essential and extremely valuable. Good governance allows companies to acquire and maintain a favourable reputation, which is paramount to long-term success. Finally, companies need to retain their core business propositions even as they adapt. If they make shifts that are too radical, they risk losing their advantages of global scale and branding. Khanna and Palepu[42] discovered that, although Dell's original business model emphasised digital ordering and minimal inventory, its direct-sales approach would not work in China as local customers still preferred a paper-based order system. Dell was smart enough to adapt its model to gain market acceptance without destroying its competitive advantage, by first offering a small range of products.

2.3 DOING BUSINESS IN AFRICA

A great tool to use when planning to enter a new market, start a business or pick a business partner is 'The Golden Circle' *(Figure 4)*, which is discussed in the book, *Start with why*.[43] A business first needs authenticity and consistency in its **what**. *What* are its products and services going to be? Next, it is vital to use verbs when describing **how** the business is going to realise its vision. *How* is it going to surpass its competitors? *How* is it going to attain sufficient market share? Finally, the **why** must speak about why that company wants to take on Africa. That *why* must be communicated from top level management down to the customer. Leadership, expatriates and members of the diaspora working for international companies in destination countries have to understand their parent company's *why*, must know what their mission is, and must understand *how* to accomplish it in the host country. Even if a company is not the first to enter the chosen market, if it has a solid conviction on why it should be there, that hunger will keep its team going when Africa challenges it. Businesses should, therefore, take time to establish and communicate their core values to all team members and other relevant participants.

AFRICA'S POTENTIAL

Africa is rich in mineral resources, with each country having specific advantages that create unique opportunities. The continent is also home to a significant amount of the world's natural resources, both renewable and non-renewable. The continent thus has huge untapped potential; both for the rest of the world and for African nationals. If the different African nations prioritised coming together to develop their potential, there is no limit to what the continent could become. Less poverty, more collaboration, improved trade and increased development would all be possible.

The creation of jobs might build local affinities towards other African nationalities. Do not be deceived, the continent would still have issues, but all great opportunities begin with a need to change a broken system or way of thinking.

Figure 4: The Golden Circle for Africa

WHY?
WHAT?
HOW?

WHY AFRICA IS A GOOD DESTINATION FOR FDI
Since the 1990s, many African countries have improved their governance and created a better business climate by building their

institutional capacities and strengthening their legal systems.[45] In addition, Africa is a dynamic continent with continuously evolving markets that can offer foreign investors different opportunities. For starters, the African Continental Free Trade Area (AfCFTA) has delivered the required openness for trade on the continent and has encouraged more greenfield investments.[46] Several developing African countries are currently producing below their potential GDP, which means that innovation can spark growth and greater returns. The sectors that most frequently attract greenfield investments are typically the manufacturing and services sectors, however other sectors, such as logistics, IT services and renewable energy, are also attracting a significant amount of interest from investors.[47] Yet while there are a variety of sectors to explore in the African setting, MNEs need to be forward-looking to determine gaps in the market and assess whether there is a way to create an edge that will help them fend off competitors and maintain profitability in the future.

SUSTAINABLE FDI OPPORTUNITIES

Investment in the African continent should ideally focus on the key sectors and opportunities that will define the continent's growth in both the short- and long-term. Investors should be looking to challenge the status quo and think differently about the landscape to achieve desired success. One of these sectors is energy, specifically renewable energy. Other prominent sectors are e-commerce and logistics. With the rise in online shopping and the infrastructure and logistical challenges that companies have not yet addressed, there is much untapped potential for foreign investment in these areas.[48] These are just a few examples of what can be investigated and implemented with the right mindset. Investors should also take note of FDI returns on capital. It is important to understand the risk-return profile of any investment and to adequately analyse the real GDP growth rates of the host country. Assessing whether the industry is profitable and the economy is growing can assist companies to choose the best FDI destination.

2.3.1 WHY IS AFRICA AN ATTRACTIVE MARKET FOR BUSINESS EXPANSION?

Africa's total population is expected to reach approximately 2.5 billion by 2050, up from 1.34 billion in 2020. Nigeria, Ethiopia and the Democratic Republic of Congo will rank as the continent's three most populous countries by then *(see Figure 5)*, with a combined population of 800 million.[49] Population is a great proxy for the size of an opportunity. If a company were to produce a product that is consumed respective to the size of the market, a large population indicates that there are more potential customers to attract. As the continent with the youngest average population in the world, as well as a large variety of social and economic issues that still need to be resolved, Africa presents a huge opportunity for creativity and innovation. For those companies with an appetite to solve problems and create sustainable solutions that change people's lives, Africa can provide the platform.

DEVELOPED COUNTRY MULTINATIONALS

Multinationals from developed countries have traditionally entered new markets that have access to contract manufacturing, service outsourcing and joint ventures. Africa, with its diverse marketplace of 54 countries, is not a 'one-size-fits-all', yet it presents an ideal opportunity for companies to understand the dynamic shifts of products or solutions using adaptive strategies to compete. Despite the internal organisational expertise that such companies have, for ventures to succeed in Africa, people need to be hired not just for the job at hand, but also for a cultural fit. This key competency assists in ensuring that the people hired will perform well over time in a given environment. Yet while such multinationals tend to hire local managers to mitigate the risk of cultural missteps, they often struggle to find staff with the relevant skills.

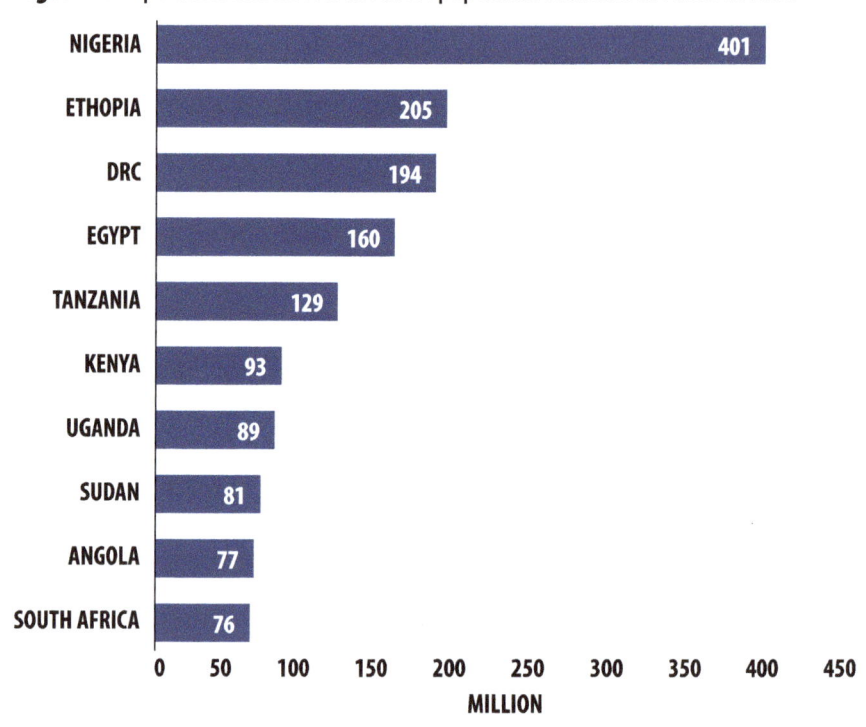

Figure 5: Population forecast for the most populated countries in Africa in 2050

Country	Population (Million)
NIGERIA	401
ETHOPIA	205
DRC	194
EGYPT	160
TANZANIA	129
KENYA	93
UGANDA	89
SUDAN	81
ANGOLA	77
SOUTH AFRICA	76

HOME-GROWN AFRICAN COMPANIES

Given the glaring institutional voids in many African countries, local businesses tend to develop capabilities for relationship-based management in their home environments, which make up for the lack of institutional infrastructure. These assets may be used domestically or abroad in other emerging markets, where such assets would likewise be useful. These home-grown African companies, such as MTN, Shoprite and Dangote Cement, by their nature show resilience when they expand into other African countries. African companies that become global giants start by expanding easily into other African markets and, over time, enter other geographic markets outside the continent.[50] Essentially, such companies use their knowledge of local customers' particular preferences to build businesses founded on distinctive national characteristics. The poorer the quality of governance in a country, the higher the number of developing country multinationals among the largest subsidiaries in that country.

According to *African Business*, market capitalisation of the top 250 African companies rose by 69% to US$710 billion year-on-year between 2020 and 2021.[51] This was at the height of the Covid-19 pandemic when global supply chains were fragmented, so it is significant. Given that previous trends did not show such huge changes, this massive growth indicates the versatility and nimbleness that CEOs and business leaders in Africa can employ in unpredictable conditions. These leaders can flourish and find ways to make their businesses successful, despite unpredictable political and economic environments.

Africa has become a 'hotbed' for South African companies. South African multinationals, with their more developed home infrastructure compared with the rest of the continent, have comparatively more resources available. These include internalised knowledge, financial resources and experience, which are key ingredients for successful internationalisation. As per *African Business*, 74% of market capitalisation in Africa comes from the Southern African region *(Figure 6)*. Most of those companies come from South Africa, which has eight of the top 10 companies and 98 of the top 250 companies.[52]

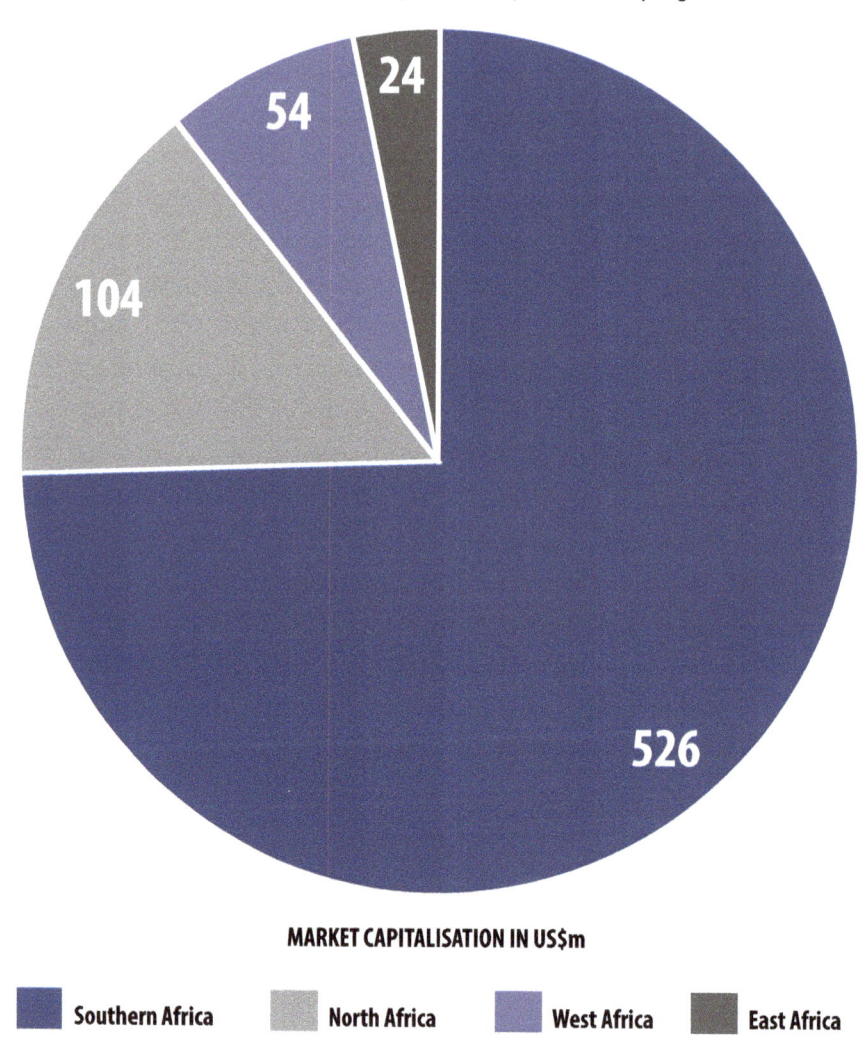

Figure 6: Africa's top 250 companies by market capitalisation by region[53]

- Southern Africa: 526
- North Africa: 104
- West Africa: 54
- East Africa: 24

MARKET CAPITALISATION IN US$m

The expansion of South African corporates onto the African continent has been one of the unheralded business successes of the past century. As the continent continues to be attractive to both large and small companies, being a first mover in a sector is the best place to be. A case in point is the growth of the mobile telephony company, MTN. Since its inception in the 1990s, it has grown to become a continental and global player in the telecommunications sector. The growth of mobile telephony has created opportunities for companies around the world to utilise technology to attain a wider reach. Documented case studies on MTN describe how the organisation has managed to succeed in Africa's emerging markets. Its achievements on the continent are largely attributed to adopting collaborative partnerships with governments and businesses, embracing Africa's diversity, and nurturing and developing Africa's human talent while providing local communities with a licence to operate. African governments welcome MTN's brand of responsible and committed investment.

2.3.2 BUSINESS MODELS USED TO EXPAND OPERATIONS ACROSS THE AFRICAN CONTINENT

The internationalisation of businesses in Africa results from three interrelated decisions: **where** to expand (country or location); **when** to expand (timing); and **how** to expand (mode of entry). While such decisions can be high-risk, the more businesses expand across borders, the more comfortable they feel and the more ownership commitment there is.

Each of the entry modes shown in *Table 2* has its own set of advantages and disadvantages. If a company decides to export, for example, its costs of setting up business in the foreign country will be lower, but it has to find ways to transport its goods to the host country and distribute them. On the other hand, partnerships and strategic alliances reduce the amount of investment that a company needs to make in the host country as these are shared with the partner, but the overall costs of partnering are much higher than exporting, and there could be integration challenges between the corporate cultures.

Table 2: Internationalisation entry modes explained

ENTRY MODE	LEVEL OF CONTROL IN HOST COUNTRY	ENTRY MODE EXPLAINED
EXPORTING	NONE	Selling goods produced in one country into one or more other countries.
LICENSING/ FRANCHISING	LOW	The owner makes limited rights or resources available (for a fee and royalties) to the licensee in the host country to manufacture a proprietor's product for a fixed term in a specific market.
PARTNERSHIPS/JOINT VENTURES	MEDIUM	Some level of control of a company in another country or the creation of a third independently managed company by two companies where the risk is shared.
WHOLLY OWNED	FULL (100%)	This is a model where the domestic company fully owns and controls the operation in the destination country. Such a model is achieved through setting up a branch in another country, the acquisition of a foreign company, or a greenfield investment.

"*For those companies with an appetite to solve problems and create sustainable solutions that change people's lives, Africa can provide the platform.*"

THREE

MARKET RESEARCH

To be successful in any business venture, market research and practical knowledge are essential to understand how things work. Once a product line or concept is developed, some companies want to present it to the market immediately, yet some scenario planning and market testing should be done first in order to understand the consumer.

Mixed method research, i.e., a combination of qualitative and quantitative research, is commonly used to gather data. This type of research can help provide a more complete picture, as it offsets the inherent weaknesses of using a single approach.

My PhD dissertation utilised this method by incorporating a survey among select South African companies doing business in Africa, followed by detailed case studies for two of those companies. My intention was to first gain insight into how these businesses expanded on the continent and what their experiences were, and second, to identify the key considerations of the companies during the various stages of internationalisation.

3.1 SURVEY OF COMPANIES DOING BUSINESS IN MULTIPLE AFRICAN COUNTRIES

A web-based, cross-sectional survey was used to collect data from select South African corporates that had operations in more than one country on the African continent, outside South Africa. The survey took the form of a questionnaire, which aimed to highlight the factors influencing each of the stages of internationalisation, provide a general understanding of what the MNEs did, and ascertain which considerations were taken into account when setting up operations in the chosen markets.

3.1.1 INTRODUCTION

The sectors of the target companies were finance, telecommunications and retail. According to Global Africa Network[54], these are the three top sectors within the rest of Africa. Some of the MNEs were listed on the Johannesburg Stock Exchange (JSE) and all had a presence in more than two countries in Africa. The survey's targeted participants were key decision-makers in senior management and people who were at least part of the decision-making team in terms of foreign investment decisions in their respective companies. These included senior strategic managers, executives, implementers of the strategy, merger and acquisitions professionals, those providing value-added services, and individuals running the foreign operations. A total of 48 respondents across 23 companies participated in the survey and answered specific sets of questions. The first tranche of questions was designed to ascertain the role of the participants in respect of planning, implementation and support. These were followed by questions regarding the extent of the respondents' companies' footprint on the continent, followed by planning, implementation and post-implementation-related questions.

3.1.2 MARKET CHOICE

A total of 14 African destination countries were selected for the research, based on the perceived ease of doing business in those countries according to the respondents from the South African companies that participated in the survey. These were mainly neighbouring countries, as well as those with larger populations and better economic outlooks. Because of cross-border migration, it was easy to find South African brands in most of these countries. Of the companies surveyed, 88.6% had been doing business in other African countries for five or more years.

3.1.3 SURVEY RESULTS AND FINDINGS

As the research was completed in 2019, the rankings could have changed, but the core messages and learnings are still valid:

> **QUESTION 1: In which African countries outside South Africa does your business have presence (can be more than one)?**

The respondents were asked to indicate the markets in which their MNEs had operations or had attempted to venture into:
- Growth markets, such as Ghana, Nigeria and Kenya, were selected by most respondents.
- Next were neighbouring countries, specifically SADC countries such as Zambia, Namibia, Eswatini, Zimbabwe and Botswana.

As per *Figure 7*, the executives indicated that their organisations operated primarily in Ghana, Kenya and Nigeria, and that South African corporates target regional growth markets as well as neighbouring countries. Growth markets are chosen because of their low economic distance and large populations. These, combined with a growing number of affluent citizens, present

3.1 SURVEY OF COMPANIES DOING BUSINESS IN MULTIPLE AFRICAN COUNTRIES

a greater opportunity for companies to realise profits. Some countries like Ethiopia and Egypt, which have small economic distances when it comes to population size, were less attractive to South African multinationals because of huge differences in culture and religion.

Figure 7: Countries where the respondents' companies were represented during their period of internationalisation

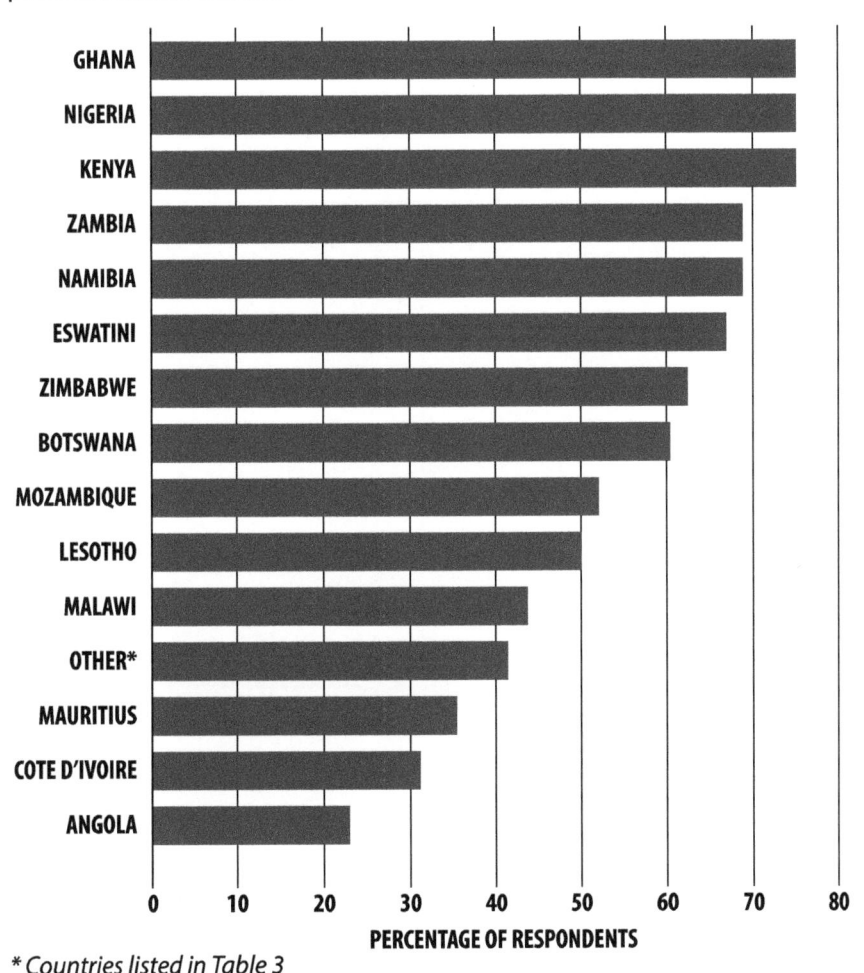

*Countries listed in Table 3

Of the countries that were not listed in the survey, but which emerged as popular host countries for South African companies, the top five were Uganda, Tanzania, the Democratic Republic of Congo, Rwanda and South Sudan.

Table 3: Other countries targeted by the respondents' companies

OTHER TARGETED COUNTRIES	NUMBER OF RESPONDENTS
UGANDA	23%
TANZANIA	16%
DRC	9%
RWANDA	9%
SOUTH SUDAN	7%
BENIN	5%
CONGO	5%
CAMEROON	4%
SUDAN	4%
SEYCHELLES	4%
EGYPT	4%
MOROCCO	2%
GABON	2%
BURKINA FASO	2%
CHAD	2%
GUINEA CONAKRY	2%
GUINEA BISSAU	2%

3.1 SURVEY OF COMPANIES DOING BUSINESS IN MULTIPLE AFRICAN COUNTRIES

For South African MNEs, the decision to enter neighbouring countries was the easiest to make as these were familiar environments. South Africa's neighbours are predominantly English-speaking, with relatively similar psychic distances, regulatory frameworks and customer tastes, making them prime destinations. An exception to this is the Portuguese-speaking countries of Mozambique and Angola, which MNEs are selective about entering. They are also cautious when entering French-speaking markets in central and West Africa, and do not usually target Arabic-speaking countries beyond sub-Saharan Africa. Looking at Angola and Mozambique in particular, despite Angola being economically attractive with natural resources like oil and gas, more South African companies have entered Mozambique as it is much closer geographically.

> **QUESTION 2: Which is the main source of data that your business uses to assess such strategic opportunities?**

Adequate resources allow companies to exploit opportunities and limit threats. One of the most priceless resources in this information age is data. In this survey, the respondents were asked to select from a list of four data sources which their businesses use most to assess market opportunities.

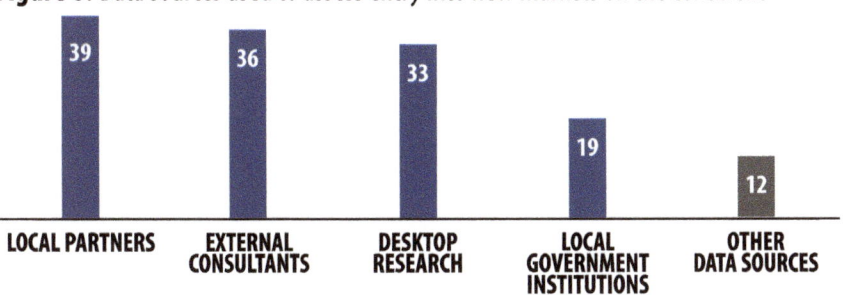

Figure 8: Data sources used to assess entry into new markets on the continent

Source	Value
LOCAL PARTNERS	39
EXTERNAL CONSULTANTS	36
DESKTOP RESEARCH	33
LOCAL GOVERNMENT INSTITUTIONS	19
OTHER DATA SOURCES	12

Reliable information facilitates efficient decision-making. Most of the respondents *(Figure 8)*, indicated that their main source of data was local partners, followed by external consultants and then desktop research. Although all external consultants are usually viewed as keepers of economic and market intelligence for local markets, it is interesting to note that when South African corporates enter these developing markets, audit companies specifically were most commonly a secondary data source.

Table 4: Other data sources

	OTHER
1	Results compared with initial budgets
2	Base analytics data
3	In-house analysts
4	Dedicated internal market intelligence function
5	Starting with a familiar product offering to gather market information
6	Client local branches
7	Vendors who directly supply those countries
8	Growth indices and expanding economic factors
9	E&Y, kPMG and PWC reports
10	Reinsurers
11	Local regulatory authorities
12	International agencies, e.g., The IMF

Internal External

3.1 SURVEY OF COMPANIES DOING BUSINESS IN MULTIPLE AFRICAN COUNTRIES

Other sources of data *(Table 4)* included vendors that directly supply information, reinsurers and internal market intelligence departments that provide and guide entry strategies. As the main methods of sourcing information will not suit all strategies, other methods of collecting information about host countries are also important. Both internal and external sources, including international bodies such as the IMF and World Bank, can supplement market intelligence.

> **QUESTION 3: Which foreign market entry mode does your business predominantly use?**

Over 70% of the respondents said that their organisations use mostly joint ventures or partnerships as their entry mode *(Figure 9)*. The joint venture entry mode is generally preferred as it presents an opportunity to set up quickly with a partner that knows the local market environment, the major players and the tastes of local customers. The least used strategy is licencing or leasing, as the risk is seen as being too high because of the loss of control of the product.

As per *Figure 9(b)*, the respondents indicated that the processes followed when deciding on internationalisation are broadly based on feasibility studies (49%), organisational group strategies (43%), and to a small extent the company following a client's strategy. Feasibility studies involve testing the model in the target market. Given the unavailability of market intelligence for prospective new entrants due to institutional voids, the respondents indicated that they have a high reliance on local partners as the main source of data used to assess strategic opportunities. For multinationals exploring opportunities on the continent, the institutional setting is not as clear as developed countries, so going into partnerships offers valuable opportunities for international businesses to increase their understanding of local business systems and forge the coexistence of such structures. The advantage of partnerships is that they potentially lessen the risk of the company being overwhelmed by foreign institutional voids, and they also provide local insights into the legal and regulatory frameworks of the host country.

Figure 9: Entry strategies used for internationalisation

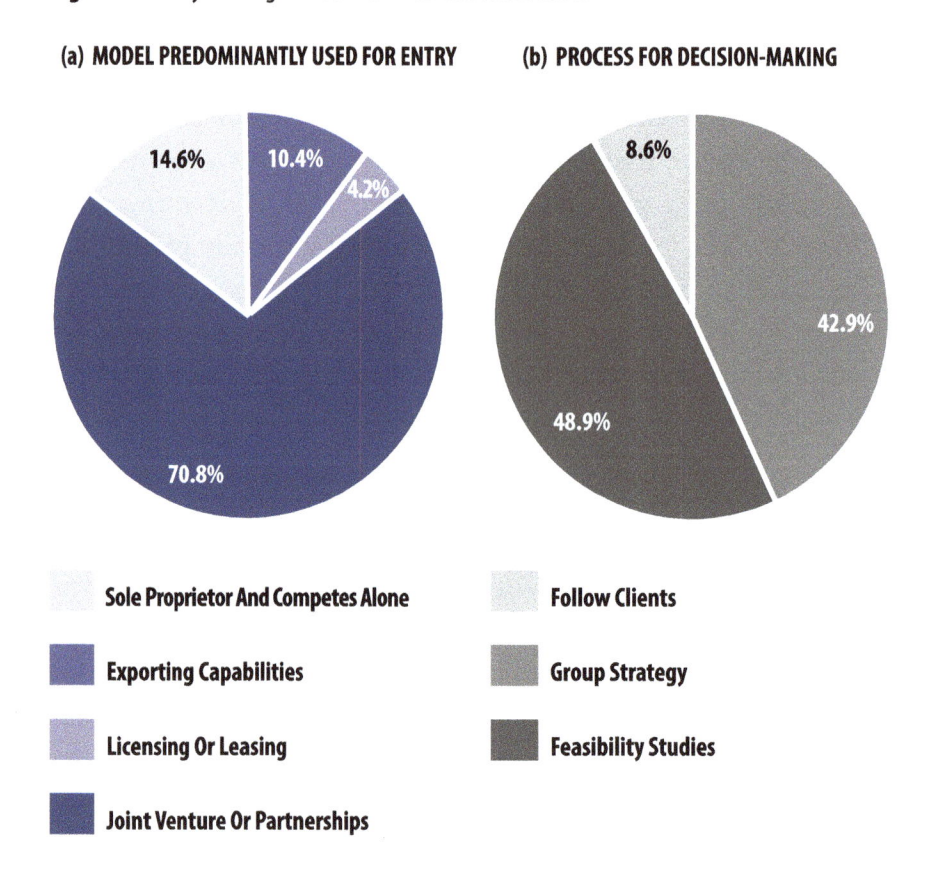

(a) MODEL PREDOMINANTLY USED FOR ENTRY

- 14.6% Sole Proprietor And Competes Alone
- 10.4% Exporting Capabilities
- 4.2% Licensing Or Leasing
- 70.8% Joint Venture Or Partnerships

(b) PROCESS FOR DECISION-MAKING

- 8.6% Follow Clients
- 42.9% Group Strategy
- 48.9% Feasibility Studies

3.1 SURVEY OF COMPANIES DOING BUSINESS IN MULTIPLE AFRICAN COUNTRIES

> **QUESTION 4: After planning, how long does it take to implement or enter the new market and start to break even?**

The respondents were asked about the time it takes to plan and implement a strategy for a new target market on the continent. The results showed that South African corporates generally take more than six months to plan an expansion into a target market, with most (66.7%) taking between six months and two years, and a further 22.9% taking more than two years.

Although over 70% of the respondents indicated that planning generally takes two years or less, they noted that implementation takes longer *(Figure 10)*. More than 55% stated that because of the uneven economic African landscape, implementing strategies in these markets takes between two and five years. Why is this? When companies internationalise, they tend to use certain indicators to gain insights into regulatory, cultural, competitive and industry-specific information. Unfortunately, as most African markets are plagued by institutional voids and therefore lack this crucial information or have outdated versions of it, inconsistencies result. Companies thus find themselves planning and implementing with insufficient information. Only during the implementation stage do these gaps or challenges start to manifest, causing the implementation process to take longer than planned. For those that complete their implementation in less than two years, this could be because of the entry mode selected, the industry, or their level of familiarity with the host country.

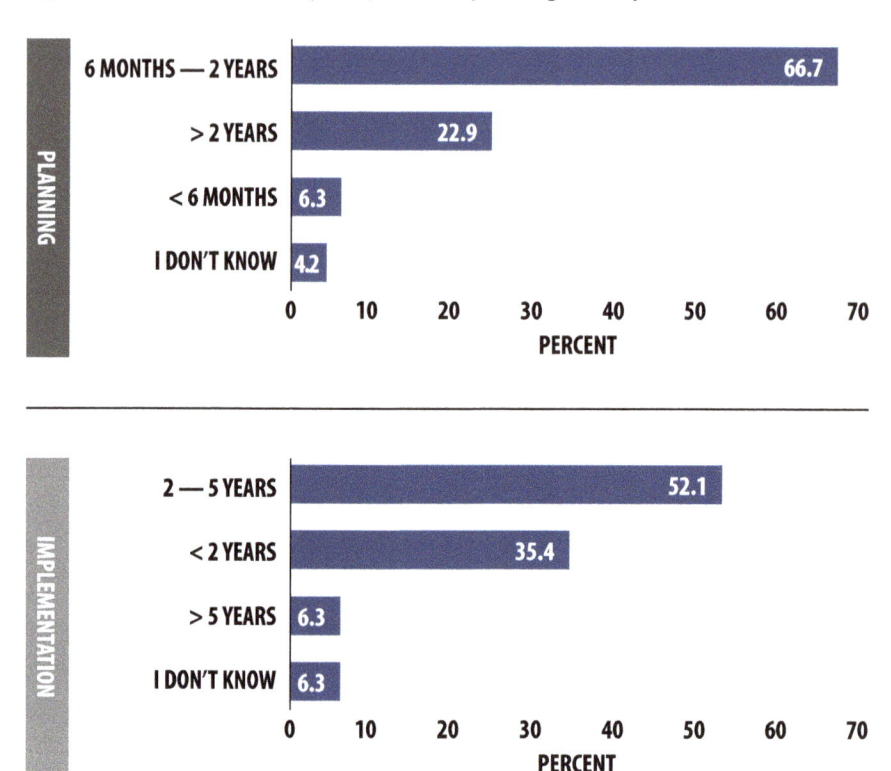

Figure 10: The time taken by companies for planning and implementation

PLANNING
- 6 MONTHS — 2 YEARS: 66.7
- > 2 YEARS: 22.9
- < 6 MONTHS: 6.3
- I DON'T KNOW: 4.2

PERCENT

IMPLEMENTATION
- 2 — 5 YEARS: 52.1
- < 2 YEARS: 35.4
- > 5 YEARS: 6.3
- I DON'T KNOW: 6.3

PERCENT

QUESTION 5: What additional considerations are used when planning for expansion into other countries?

Considerations for corporates on whether to expand their operations outside their national borders largely depend on the opportunities available to grow their businesses. Some respondents listed additional considerations used during planning, with seven of those highlighting market opportunities as an important consideration *(Figure 11)*. The other two flagged regulatory constraints.

Figure 11: Other considerations used for planning processes

QUESTION 6: Has your strategy failed in any of your chosen markets?

When reflecting on the internationalisation strategies after operations were set up in the preferred locations, the respondents indicated that some plans succeeded although they took longer than expected. In addition, even after careful planning, some of the strategies did not meet the set expectations *(Figure 12)*.

Figure 12: Outcomes of internationalisation strategies

- **6%** Exceeded expectations
- **73%** Somewhat exceeded expectations
- **21%** Failed to meet expectations

An encouraging 79% of the respondents stated that their company strategies succeeded. Although expectations were met in the targeted geographic markets, the large number of 'Somewhat exceeded expectations' is a sign that there is a level of uncertainty that cannot be planned for. Learning from experience helps businesses to detect risks early and to manage them by customising their strategies, leading to better outcomes.

> **QUESTION 7: If a strategy failed, what were the root causes?**

When asked why their companies failed in certain markets, the most cited cause was 'copying and pasting' the strategy used in South Africa to the target country, i.e., the company did not take the varying landscape of the destination market into account. In the words of one respondent, '...this boiled down to a lack of understanding of the local environment and how significantly it differs from South Africa *(Figure 13)*. Other significant failures were attributed to regulatory challenges, changes in market conditions, implementation taking longer than expected and cultural distance.

Success in African countries entails making the right choice at the right time, but this is only possible if an MNE conducts its due diligence thoroughly. Included in this is an understanding of the target market, as well as adequately profiling and valuing the target customer. Businesses that lead with empathy and genuinely address the needs of their customers also build loyal client relationships[55] and offer better products. The logic behind this is to look at all angles of what you are trying to develop according to the perspective of the client; consider their viewpoint to try and see what value your company is bringing them. Market research, empathy and being aware of biases are key mechanisms to identify risks and avoid failure.

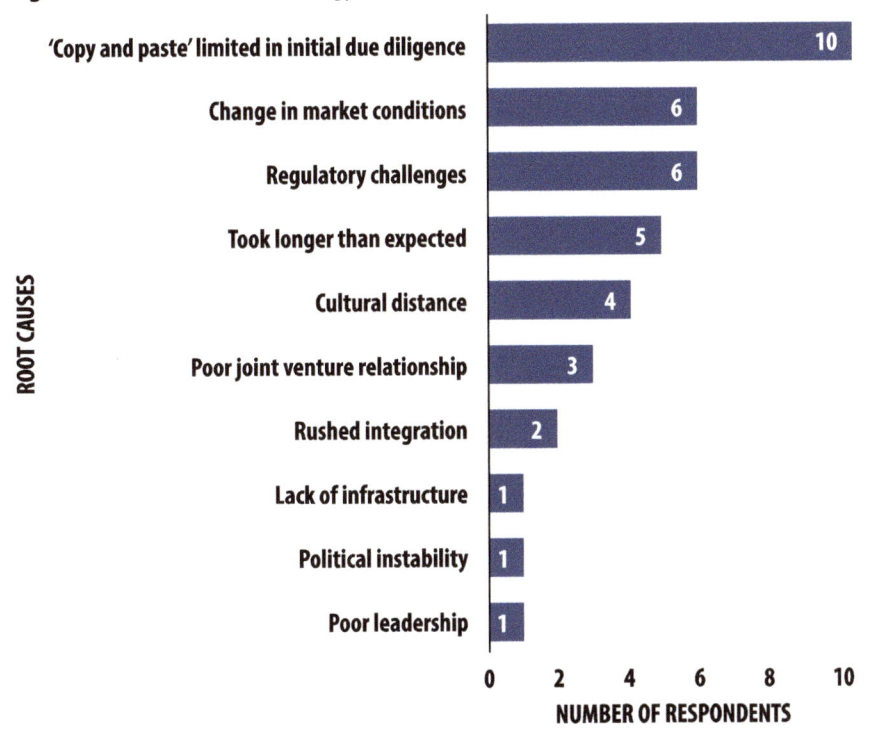

3.1 SURVEY OF COMPANIES DOING BUSINESS IN MULTIPLE AFRICAN COUNTRIES

Figure 13: Root causes of strategy failures

Root cause	Number of respondents
'Copy and paste' limited in initial due diligence	10
Change in market conditions	6
Regulatory challenges	6
Took longer than expected	5
Cultural distance	4
Poor joint venture relationship	3
Rushed integration	2
Lack of infrastructure	1
Political instability	1
Poor leadership	1

QUESTION 8: Is your company addressing the root causes of the above failure? If not, why?

There are two constants in almost every market: the risk of failure and change. When things are not going as planned, there are both good and bad ways of responding. The participants were asked to specify what their companies had done in the face of failure.

Of the 28 respondents who answered this question, most stated that adapting their original strategies and having the conviction to make them work gave their companies hope of staying afloat. The secret to winning in the long run lies in knowing what to forget and what to create.[56] Making a huge upfront investment also acts as a deterrent to giving up and exiting the market. Being agile, innovative and flexible serves companies well in this fast-changing world. This is why it is important to remember that not everything will go as planned, and sometimes, the worst-case scenario may come to pass. If we have learnt anything from the winners, it is that mindset and patience can take you a long way.

Figure 14: Strategic decisions that companies take when they face challenges in certain markets

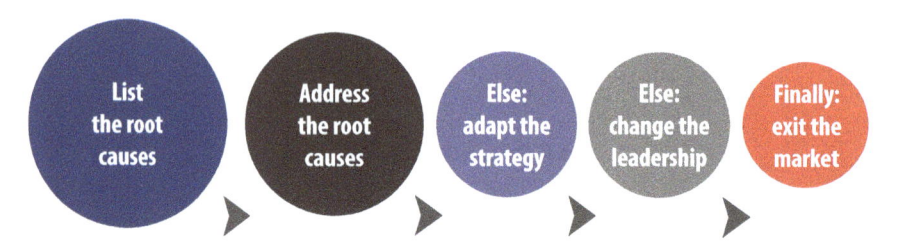

- List the root causes
- Address the root causes
- Else: adapt the strategy
- Else: change the leadership
- Finally: exit the market

> **QUESTION 9:** Looking back at the challenges you had when setting up your operation in a foreign country, on a scale of 1 to 5, how have the considerations below attributed to your success?

What did successful companies do to win on the continent? It was not surprising that the respondents rated 'Successful implementation of strategy in the identified markets' as their company's highest achievement, followed closely by 'Robust planning before entering the new market', 'How quickly the company responded when market conditions changed' and 'Being able to accurately assess and size the opportunity'.

Throughout the survey, the respondents emphasised the importance of understanding the cultures and norms of the destination country, and of having the right leaders in place to guide the company to find its way in these new market dynamics. In principle, it is investing a little and learning a lot to accurately assess

3.1 SURVEY OF COMPANIES DOING BUSINESS IN MULTIPLE AFRICAN COUNTRIES

the market. It will probably be more challenging to do that without precise information upfront, but flexible plans and agile responses can alleviate some uncertainties and will eventually bring the right customers knocking to buy into the vision of the business.

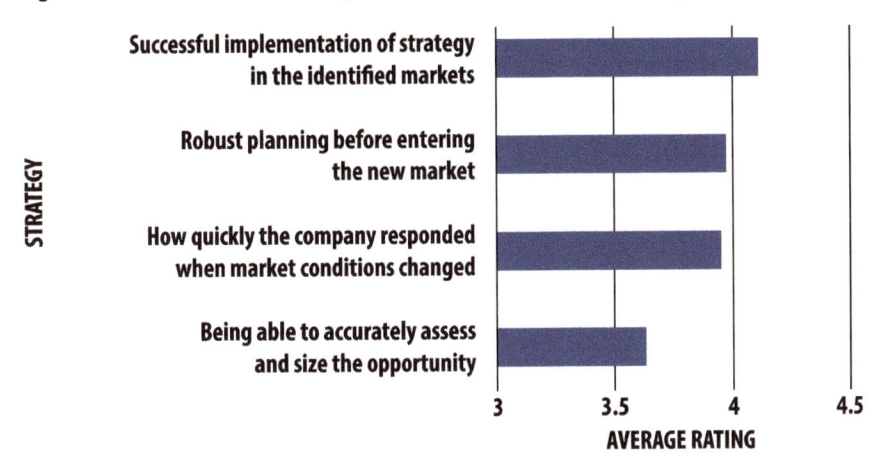

Figure 15: Successes of the companies' internationalisation strategies

STRATEGY
- Successful implementation of strategy in the identified markets
- Robust planning before entering the new market
- How quickly the company responded when market conditions changed
- Being able to accurately assess and size the opportunity

AVERAGE RATING (3 – 4.5)

> **QUESTION 10:** The following considerations are used when planning for expansion into other countries. For your business, on a scale from 1-5, please rate the significance that each of the below made on your decision to choose your frontier market.

The participants were asked to rate why their companies pursued their internationalisation strategies. The responses showed that 'Taking a long-term view' was the most common, followed by 'Infrastructure availability', 'Leadership with international experience', 'Finding the right local talent' and 'Ease of exportation of strategy' *(Figure 16)*. Multinational firms that have decided to be pioneers in emerging markets should expect difficulties, because while the need for non-market resources is high, these take time to build. The African market conditions that are significantly different from one country to the next can work in favour or against such multinationals. Though it might be easy to enter certain markets, the next country's market conditions could be completely different, so consideration of a first mover strategy in such markets should be accompanied by a deep understanding of the market's economic, technological, social, cultural, regulatory and competitive conditions. Measures must thus be taken to overcome difficulties and a long-term view must be adopted to allow for countries to acquire experience to successfully compete in such markets.

Figure 16: Ratings of key considerations for internationalisation

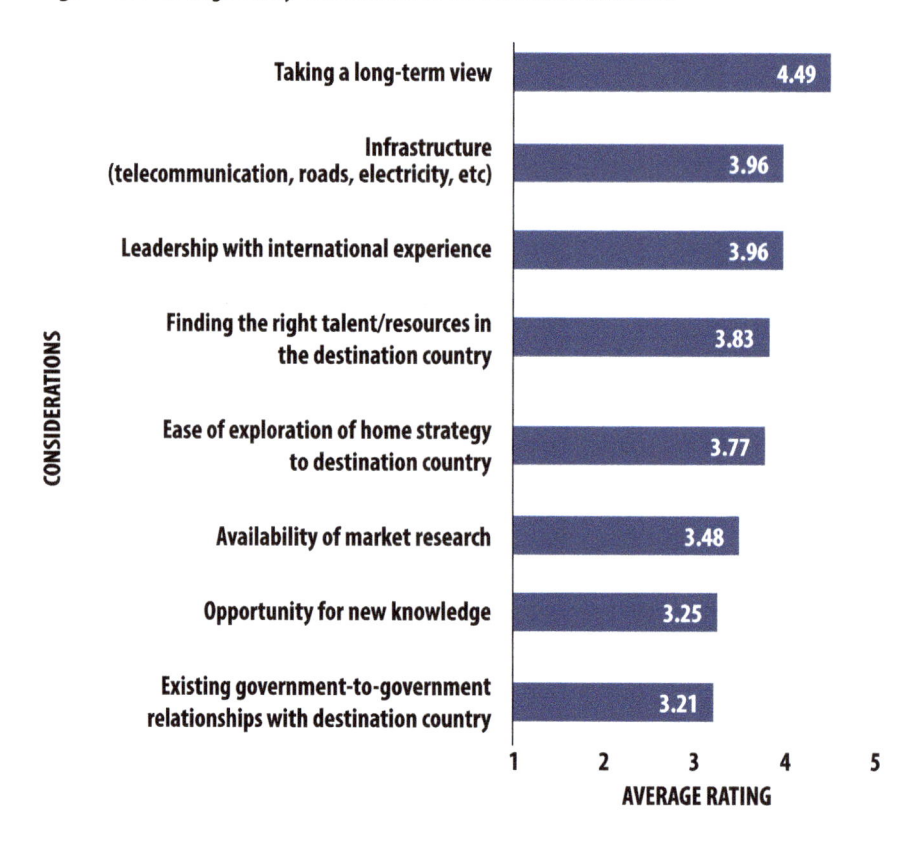

Considerations	Average Rating
Taking a long-term view	4.49
Infrastructure (telecommunication, roads, electricity, etc)	3.96
Leadership with international experience	3.96
Finding the right talent/resources in the destination country	3.83
Ease of exploration of home strategy to destination country	3.77
Availability of market research	3.48
Opportunity for new knowledge	3.25
Existing government-to-government relationships with destination country	3.21

'Existing government-to-government relationships with destination country' was, unsurprisingly, the lowest rated consideration, as corporates focus on business opportunities and not necessarily on political favours. Given the political volatility in some African countries, having good government-to-government relationships is not seen as that valuable; political dynamics can change quickly and there would not be anything the home country could do to manage the risk. 'Opportunity for new knowledge' was also not rated highly, as this could be mitigated by a joint venture or partnership with local partners who would provide the required knowledge.

> **QUESTION 11:** In the countries where your internationalisation strategy was successful, on a scale of 1 to 5, please rate how the following considerations directly influenced your success?

The respondents were also asked to rate specific in-country factors that could have contributed to their successes in the destination markets *(Figure 17)*. The most highly rated factor was 'Taking a long-term view', followed by 'Leadership with international experience' and 'Finding the right talent/resources in the destination country'. It was not surprising to see 'Taking a long-term view' as the top consideration, given the uneven market conditions in the varying destination countries.

African market conditions differ significantly from one country to the next, which can work in favour of, or against, emerging market pioneers. Although it might be easy to enter certain markets, the next country's market conditions could be completely different. Having a deep understanding of a market's economic, technological, social, regulatory and competitive conditions makes the landing a little gentler. Thriving in changing conditions can only happen if companies immerse themselves in what makes that country tick. What are their cultures and people like? How do they do business? What is missing from the market? For example, the Democratic Republic of Congo, which has a larger market size and is geographically closer to South Africa than countries such as Nigeria, Ghana and Kenya, as well as being part of the same regional economic bloc (SADC), is not as popular a target market with South African MNEs as one might expect. This is chiefly because of the language difference. A different language presents an additional cost, while a common language facilitates internationalisation as it is central to business communication and service delivery.

Figure 17: Factors that contributed to success in the respective markets

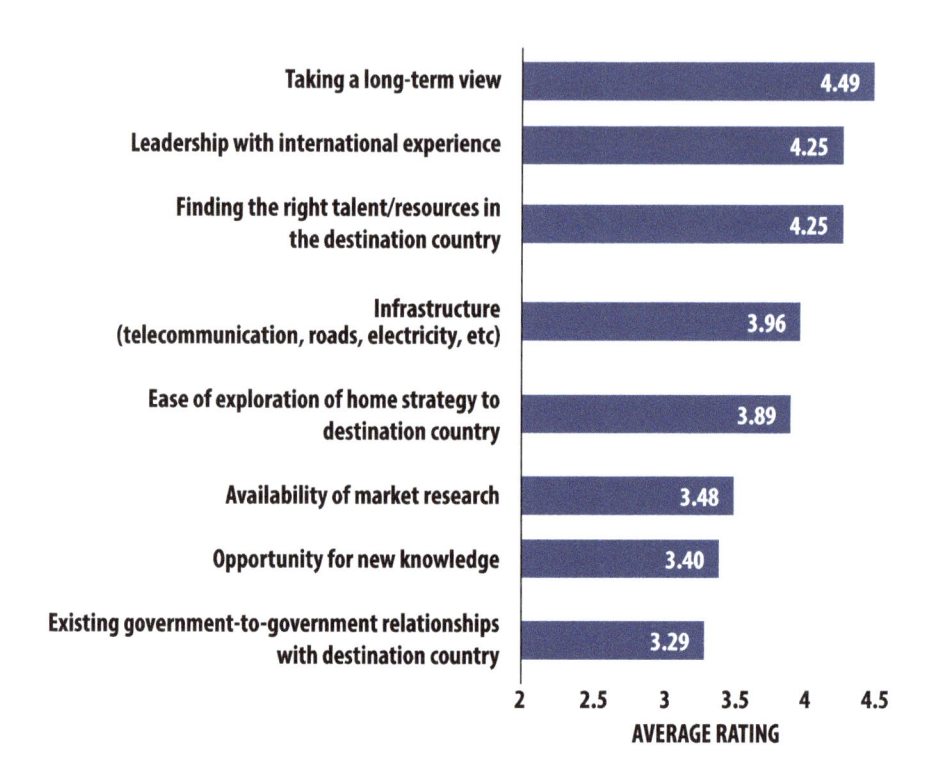

Factor	Average Rating
Taking a long-term view	4.49
Leadership with international experience	4.25
Finding the right talent/resources in the destination country	4.25
Infrastructure (telecommunication, roads, electricity, etc)	3.96
Ease of exploration of home strategy to destination country	3.89
Availability of market research	3.48
Opportunity for new knowledge	3.40
Existing government-to-government relationships with destination country	3.29

3.1 *SURVEY OF COMPANIES DOING BUSINESS IN MULTIPLE AFRICAN COUNTRIES*

> **QUESTION 12:** What does your organisation use to mitigate HR capabilities and capacity constraints in a foreign market?

Figure 18: Alignment of strategy during implementation

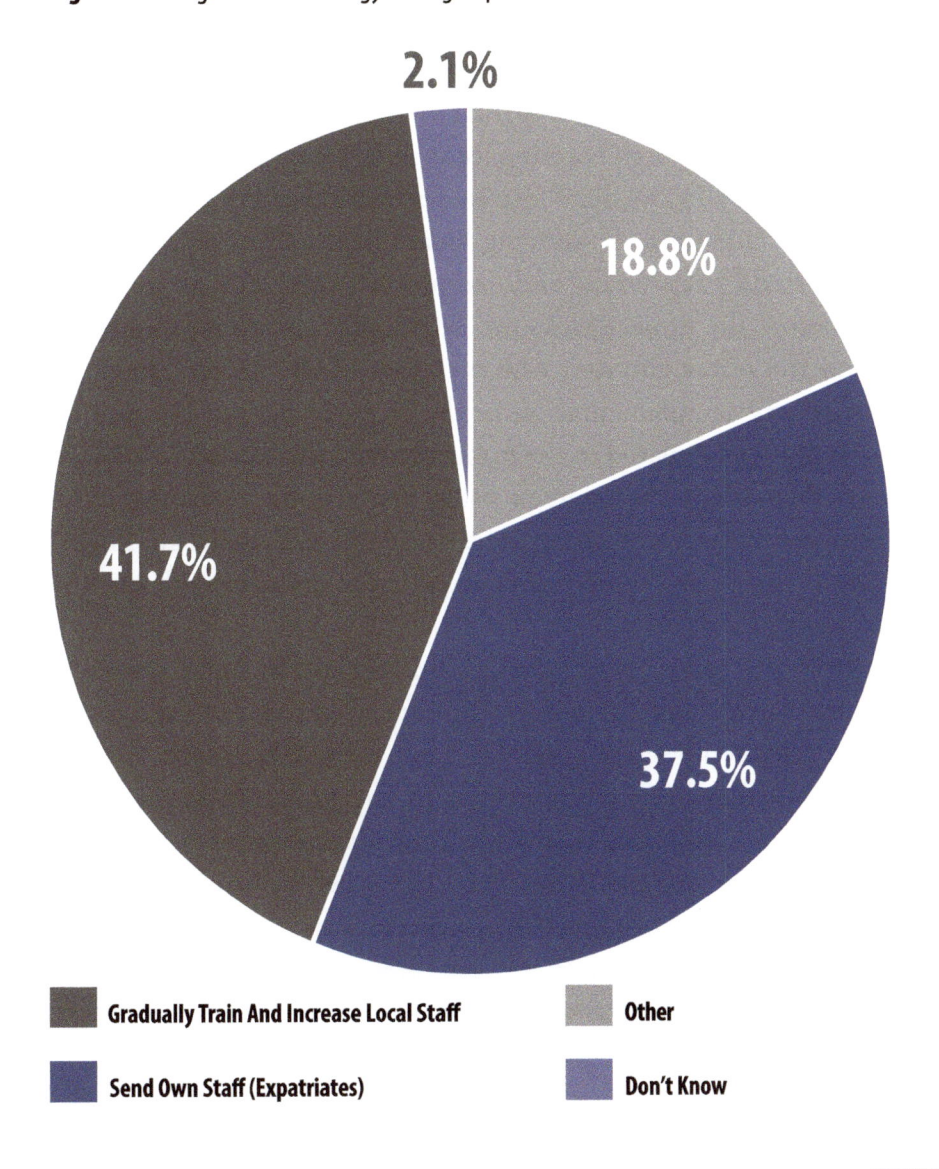

- 2.1%
- 18.8%
- 37.5%
- 41.7%

Legend:
- Gradually Train And Increase Local Staff
- Send Own Staff (Expatriates)
- Other
- Don't Know

The respondents were asked what their organisations use to ease human resources requirements *(Figure 18)*, and capacity constraints in foreign markets. The responses showed that the dominant model is to localise the operation and gradually train and increase local staff numbers. In some cases, however, corporates would send their own staff to the target country as expatriates.

Some respondents indicated that their organisations use the two models together, i.e., they use their own staff when the project starts but scale up through training local staff. One of the respondents stated: 'Initially we send expats for the mission's critical roles, with the intention of sourcing local talent as succession. This is supported by resourcing and manpower strategies that are signed off before the project kicks off.' It is important to have someone from the home country, who was part of the vision, champion the strategy implementation in the targeted nation. Because the strategy is formulated in the home country, an expatriate manager can then adapt the strategy using the acquired learnings from the host country. Alternatively, as an olive branch, an EMNE can make use of people from a diaspora to connect with the host country's locals.

Even if a company has enough human and financial resources, Rome wasn't built in a day! Building a brand can take longer than expected because goodwill is not earned overnight. After an operation has been implemented in the preferred location, the respondents indicated that while some plans succeeded, they took longer than expected. And even after careful planning, some of the strategies did not meet their expectations.

QUESTION 13: Where your entry strategy failed in your target market, what were the root causes?

Although about 30% of the interviewees indicated that their strategies succeeded in the target markets, and 10% exited the markets where they failed, the remaining 60% noted that they had adapted or were adapting their strategies to make it work:

- *'Our existence in those markets depend on it. Our clients cannot be left high and dry in any of the countries where they operate.'*
- *'Limited attention. Decision may have been short-sighted at the time. Company is undergoing strategic directional change at this time. Focus on local private label brands, versus Africa focus.'*
- *'Yes, alternative financing model through China. Vendor finance for construction.'*
- *'The causes are endogenous to the company.'*
- *'Regulatory requirements and environment are critical to the success of our business. Where the framework does not allow for us to operate with a degree of independence we stay away and explore other territories.'*
- *'Currently, taking a step-by-step approach to resolve issues and improve business.'*
- *'Management time is being spent on addressing growth and ensuring that plans and targets are met.'*
- *'As revenue grows you reinvest and then penetrate more.'*
- *'Through liaising with government where possible.'*
- *'Having local staff and partners help us to understand the market better before making huge investments. Finding local talent and investing in their development is key.'*
- *'Ensure mandates are appropriate and enforceable.'*
- *'Yes certainly, we are re-looking at the entire product strategy and go-to-market approach. As cost is an extremely sensitive factor, we are re-looking at the value for money proposition. One of the key factors is that digital migration for most*

countries has not happened as yet, except for Namibia and Kenya. This provides valuable insight into consumer behaviours on digital uptake.'
- *'Where it is regulation, it has been out of our control and we haven't been able to have certain items reviewed.'*

3.2 CASE STUDIES OF INTERNATIONALISING COMPANIES

3.2.1 INTRODUCTION

To get deeper understanding of internationalisation strategies used by South African companies as they track north in search of business opportunities, case studies were considered. The companies identified were from the financial services industry as most respondents were from the sector. The companies were chosen according to their broad footprints in their respective industry sub-sectors, when compared with their peers. The two companies were Sanlam, the largest insurance company in Africa, and Standard Bank, the biggest lender by assets in Africa.

As the aim of the study was to look at the steps the companies considered during planning, implementation and post-implementation, the case study questions were structured to gather information on the processes these companies used when expanding their businesses into other African nations, based on the on *Figure 19* below.

Figure 19: Factors that contributed to success in the respective markets

The study specifically looked at how measures such as psychic distance, firm resources and strategic choice impacted the planning and implementation of businesses in the chosen markets.

3.2.2 THE PARTNERSHIP-BASED INTERNATIONALISATION MODEL
SANLAM

The first case study company, Sanlam[57], provides financial solutions to individual and institutional clients, with solutions ranging from life insurance to general insurance, asset management and many more. The solutions that it offers in other African countries are in the main long-term insurance and general insurance. Although Sanlam uses a broad range of distribution channels in South Africa, across the continent, the bancassurance model and tied advisors are the channels it most commonly uses. (bancassurance is an arrangement between a bank and an insurance company that allows the insurance company to sell its products to the bank's clients.)

Sanlam began its expansion after the acquisition of a niche emerging market player. This acquisition had a footprint in five neighbouring countries and had internalised knowledge of expanding outside South Africa's borders. Sanlam's initial internationalisation attempts, based on desktop research and market analysis, pointed to Nigeria and Uganda as being the first frontier markets. A partner was found in Nigeria, but the company could not find a suitable purchase in Uganda. This led to them entering the country through a greenfield investment. As Africa is broadly an emerging market, it was the acquirer's internalised knowledge of the mass market insurance business that became its launching pad into African markets. At the time of writing, Sanlam was in 35 countries and had the most extensive insurance footprint on the African continent. Given their ambition to be the leading insurer on the continent, I would not be surprised if their footprint spreads even wider.

Unlike other leading South African insurance corporates, Sanlam prefers strategic partnerships in the markets the company chooses to operate in. This strategy saw the contribution of the emerging market business to the group's operating profit grow from 9% in 2010 to 21% in 2017. This success is demonstrated in its financials, which showed a contribution of 26% from businesses outside South Africa in 2017. As South Africa's biggest insurance company, Sanlam now has the most extensive insurance footprint on the African continent in pursuit of 'Pan-African dominance'. As one of the most rapidly expanding South African companies on the continent, Sanlam is also the fastest growing insurance business in Nigeria.[58] Since 2021, Sanlam has partnered with the largest mobile operator in Africa, MTN, which gives it access to more than 100 million active mobile money users. This is enabling the company to take full advantage of the growth opportunities for digital services in Africa.

3.2.3 THE OWNERSHIP-BASED INTERNATIONALISATION MODEL STANDARD BANK

The second case study, Standard Bank[59], is a major African bank and financial services group that focuses on servicing individuals, businesses and corporates. The bank is the largest banking group in South Africa in terms of assets held and is also considered Africa's largest lender by assets. For operations outside South Africa, the bank trades as Stanbic Bank, to avoid confusion with the former parent (and now competitor), Standard Chartered. Its internationalisation approach, both within South Africa and on the rest of the continent, is to leverage the strengths of all its internal capabilities and to ensure that its clusters and subsidiaries collaborate in the respective geographies to extract maximum value. Standard Bank's expansion on the continent has been more of a step approach. The bank pegged itself in South Africa in 1862, before expanding into other SADC countries and select East African countries in the early 1900s. Only in the early 20th century did it expand beyond these two regions. Its strategy was deliberate expansion through the acquisition of other banks in neighbouring countries, as well as targeting historically English colonies. This experience capacitated the bank with an understanding of the strategies required for sustainable growth and continued dominance on the continent. The company's internalised continental experience and the extensive markets it operates in on the continent made it an ideal choice for a case study.

After expanding into other markets in Europe and South America, the company refocussed its strategy back on Africa with the intention of dominating the continent. It did this by shifting its focus from core transactional and liability banking to higher-value middle-income and affluent personal and commercial customers. The company now has an on-the-ground presence in 20 countries in sub-Saharan Africa, primarily SADC countries. Beyond SADC, the organisation has targeted growth markets in regional hubs like Nigeria and Kenya, which continue to evolve and grow. Part of the group's strategy for expansion was to enter a digital partnership in 2021, which led it to partner with one of the largest fintech companies in Africa, Flutterwave, to offer easier methods of payment for clients in South Africa and Namibia. In the future, the group intends to take advantage of Africa's growing population and the ease of trade benefits from the AfCFTA, which will offer a backdrop for growth in financial and non-financial services.

3.2.4 COMPARATIVE ANALYSIS OF OWNERSHIP-BASED VS. PARTNERSHIP-BASED MODELS

Growth on the continent forms part of the core strategies for both these South African companies. One aims to have an 'unrivalled Pan-African footprint with a diversified tailored offering' through horizontal integration, while the other desires to be the 'leading financial services organisation in, for and across Africa' using vertical integration. Their appetite and tenacity to succeed on the continent are obvious, making them an ideal choice in this attempt to understand how South African corporates plan and implement their strategies on the continent *(Figure 20)*.

Figure 20: The positioning of the case study companies in internationalisation

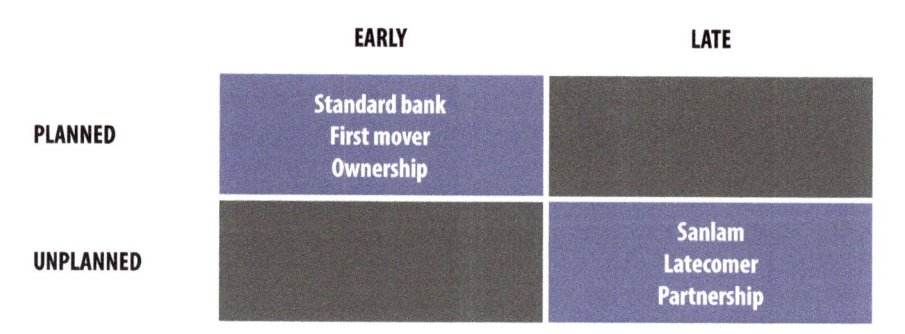

	EARLY	LATE
PLANNED	Standard bank First mover Ownership	
UNPLANNED		Sanlam Latecomer Partnership

The first mover, Standard Bank, uses the ownership model to internationalise when targeting growth markets. Standard Bank uses its experiential knowledge and dynamic capabilities to localise its subsidiaries in the host countries and can thus afford a higher level of risk. The company has had operations on the continent since the 18th century, initially targeting neighbouring countries and English-speaking growth markets. Over time it has used its experiential learnings both globally and on the African continent to expand its operations and dominate in Africa.

3.2 CASE STUDIES OF INTERNATIONALISING COMPANIES

The latecomer, Sanlam, uses the partnership model and initially language (English) to determine its target locations. Where it is not possible to partner with an English-speaking country, Sanlam considers a partner with similar values. This is the case with one of its largest partners, Allianz, which operates predominantly in French-speaking countries. The company began internationalising in 2005, so is still fairly new to internationalisation and is still expanding into multiple destinations. The insurer has a lower risk tolerance than Standard Bank, as is reflected in its approach and emphasis on focus planning to ensure minimal strategic failures.

Below are the questions asked and and qualitative summary of some of the information gathered during the interviews held with leadership as part of the case study research. While 10 people in each of the two organisations were interviewed to share their views on their organisation's internationalisation journey, selected comments from five respondents each from the two organisations have been shared to elaborate on some of the realities on the ground. (Names used are pseudonyms.)

SANLAM	Heidi	Andre	Christiaan	Leon	Kabanga
STANDARD BANK	Busi	Ibrahim	Jarred	Anne	Matthew

QUESTION 1: How did you decide which countries on the African continent to enter first?

Table 5 helps to track the steps taken by the two multinationals as they internationalised across Africa.

Table 5: Choice of markets for the two companies

SANLAM: RESPONSES	
English speaking first	67%
French speaking partner	33%

STANDARD BANK: RESPONSES	
Growth markets	62%
English speaking first	19%
Choice of markets not influenced by language	12%
Key French speaking market	8%

The two companies in the study show that distance-reducing commonalities such as economic, linguistic, cultural and institutional factors play a huge role in selecting locations for internationalising. Sanlam's choice of markets has been driven primarily by language, English being the main preference, followed by French. On the other hand, Standard Bank's choice of markets has been primarily driven by the size of the markets, specifically growth markets, followed by language.

NEIGHBOURING COUNTRIES

Both companies started internationalisation close to home in other SADC countries, despite having to navigate language barriers in Mozambique and Angola. The companies felt comfortable choosing markets that were psychically and culturally similar to their home markets.[60]

Explaining this, Heidi said:
'What you might find is that our neighbouring countries, with many people migrating in and out of South Africa, their culture has moved across borders into Lesotho, Botswana, Namibia, Zimbabwe, etc.'

Familiarity with the people and cultures in neighbouring countries makes it easier for companies to introduce suitable products and services. When psychic distance is closer, companies are able to do this because they possess knowledge of how business is conducted in such neighbouring markets. Executives of South African businesses favour entering markets closer to home because it is less costly as relevant information can be easily interpreted, making it simpler to adjust the strategy.[61]

THE ROLE OF ENGLISH IN DECISION-MAKING

Using English as a consideration for expansion beyond neighbouring countries presents some form of familiarity for both corporates. Standard Bank's growth markets in sub-Saharan Africa are English-speaking, creating familiarity for the corporate, while Sanlam has a French partner in West Africa.

Andre pointed out the importance of English as a language of instruction:

'We started out in the countries because of language. So, phase 1, English-speaking countries was a requirement because I can go there, I can meet the regulator, I can speak the language, I can read the documentation. Once I go beyond English-speaking countries, because I don't speak French, it's a lot more complicated. I can't speak to the regulators. I can't even read the acts of parliament. So, you can do it but it is more difficult.'

Cross-border expansion requires a parent company to familiarise itself with the institutional setting, thus a similar language is a common mental tool through which people make sense of an environment.

GROWTH MARKETS

The respondents from Standard Bank acknowledged that large markets, such as Nigeria with over 16% of the continent's population, cannot be ignored. Despite possible economic challenges due to the volatility of oil prices, it is a regional giant in ECOWAS and competes fiercely with South Africa as a continental giant.

Busi stated:

'It's just the size; it's too big to ignore. It's one of the biggest economies in Africa and is growing. It will continue and in fact the projection is instead of SA catching up to Nigeria, SA will end up half the size of the Nigerian economy. And again, you follow your customers... any business bank customer who has the ability to go cross border cannot ignore Nigeria. So if your customers are going there, as a bank, you have to be there. And not just our African customers, it's European customers, Asian customers, Americans. Customers know that Nigeria is too important, too big a market, irrespective of the issues and challenges they have. So as a bank, it's natural that we know that that's where our customers will gravitate and we have to be there to serve them.'

Before they make significant FDI decisions, executives need to consider consumer index factors, such as per capita incomes, lifestyles and consumer preferences in a foreign market.[62] The respondents confirmed that clients on the rest of the continent are mostly entry-level, with a small layer of wealthy clients at the top. The strategy for EMNEs should thus be to target larger markets like Nigeria, Kenya and Uganda, where the huge populations presents a bigger potential for more people to consume more global products at a given level of market penetration.

Other reasons why large emerging markets are targeted include extending a product's life cycle with new market segments or developing and launching new products.[63] To counteract the fact that it is difficult to determine potential market size, a company should have a good quality product and use different pricing strategies to test demand elasticity. This is where spending time in these markets and gathering experiential knowledge can bridge the gap.

> **QUESTION 2: What data sources do you use to assist in your planning?**

Although the two organisations use different sources of information, it is interesting to note that for both multinationals, the primary source of information when expanding into African markets is data on local dynamics *(Table 6)*. Sanlam, because it uses the partnership model and relies a lot on the value systems of its partners, invests time in understanding and learning about the internationalisation landscape and identifying the right partner. In contrast, Standard Bank, which invests time in learning about the markets in which it sets up operations, focuses on indices that can give intel to inform the economic business landscape. This enables it to gather internalised knowledge about the different markets on the continent.

What is also apparent about Sanlam is that it uses local industry players to enhance its knowledge of local markets. Internationalisation requires learning and adaptation, so, for Standard Bank, experience in these markets has shown the importance of taking control of the information rather than depending on third parties. The company has recognised the need to strengthen its internal research capacity and does due diligence when assessing operations. These are considerations that enable sounder decision-making.

Table 6: Sources of information during planning

SANLAM: RESPONSES	
Invest time into understanding local dynamics	40%
Learn by doing small deals	27%
Local industry players	24%
Desktop research	5%
Best available information	4%

STANDARD BANK: RESPONSES	
Invest time into understanding local dynamics	33%
Internal research department	20%
Economic indicators	20%
Due diligence	17%
Invest in doing homework	10%

LEARN BY DOING SMALL DEALS

Beginning with small deals reduces some of the risks of the internationalisation process in dynamic markets.[64] In its quest to become 'the pan-African insurer', the latecomer, Sanlam, refined its internationalisation processes by doing small deals to grow its Africa coverage.

Kabanga explained:
'The first deal we did in Nigeria was very small because it was a start-up. Then we did one in Malawi, which was only a few million rands. Then towards the end, we started doing bigger deals. In Rwanda, it was, I could say R100m to R200m. And this one was eventually R400m.'

This was confirmed by Christiaan, who said:
'We learnt our lessons on the small ones so that when the big one came along, we already knew how to go about it. We already had good relationships with our advisors, our lawyers,

our accountants to do the due diligence. Our team internally had experienced quite a few mistakes in the past in putting deals together.'

Emerging markets present opportunities for multinationals to sharpen their competitive responses, arbitraging learning between markets and learning how to manage and expand in a staged approach.

INVEST TIME IN UNDERSTANDING LOCAL DYNAMICS
Spending time gathering data was overwhelmingly mentioned by managers from both companies as playing a key role in internationalisation. Building an accurate source of data to make good decisions in a foreign country with large institutional voids shows commitment.

Leon stated:
'Take time and effort and spend money to understand the local market. Understand the local nuances and then go in and say, "Given what we know about insurance...", then the broader understanding of the market and the nuances and the conditions and the needs of the clients; that is how we are going to build a successful and sustainable business.'

Leon further noted:
'Get information and get it from credible sources, not from just anyone.'

> **QUESTION 3: What process do you follow in your planning?**

During the planning process, while Sanlam prioritises market analyses, Standard Bank focuses on how to dominate the markets they are in through growth *(Table 7)*. As a latecomer, Sanlam also spends time on feasibility studies and evaluating business opportunities. Because of its international experience in these markets, Standard Bank does not do this. Sanlam uses a staged approach to its internationalisation strategy as it is still trying to make sense of the nuances and to take a long-term view. Standard Bank's lengthy history on the continent is again the main reason for its wealth of tangible information, however it tests and checks before settling on a market.

Table 7: Process followed during planning

SANLAM: RESPONSES		STANDARD BANK: RESPONSES	
Market analysis	38%	Strategy is to dominate the african market	35%
Feasibility study	23%	Business case	22%
Business opportunity	16%	Feasibility study	21%
Take a long term view	13%	Follow clients	12%
Opportunity for value creation	11%	Leadership international experience and awareness	9%

As it is important to get local independent information, Heidi explained:

'So in doing the acquisition we always go and speak to the Ernst & Youngs and the PWCs. So your audit firms, speak to the banks. The banks are front runners in terms of getting a presence there. And because we have got stronger relationships with certain banks in South Africa that have entered the market, it makes it quicker when you enter the market.'

Matthew also shared that:

'It's not an area I have dealt with, but if you look at UN data, local country [data], there is data when you look around. You start by looking at local market data and what's published. You find stuff often published on the local insurance regulator if they exist. In most cases they do. Most regulators are on the internet, on annual reports, etc. It's often two years out of date, but it covers the companies that are active, the market size, all sorts, and a lot of information. Even the regulator has various information; let's say someone like the Kenyan regulator... in some cases one gets data that is three years old. It is very hard on summaries, but it's information.'

FOLLOW CLIENTS

The best opportunity for success for companies that want to pursue the ownership model is to follow their large clients and continue to service them across borders. Standard Bank uses its strong home ties with such clients to enter new markets, creating an opportunity to learn about the market while servicing the client. Once the commercial side of the bank sets up operations, it becomes a source of market intelligence on the regulatory environment, competitor information and other areas. The bank then uses this capability to set up its retail network. This creates opportunities for the bank to continue supporting its original client while also acquiring new ones. The costs of establishing the business are thus lower, as the client has done the groundwork, such as liaising with the government and knowing the competitors and the local customers.

Jarred stressed:

'With corporate and investment banking, typically from the first time we ventured into Africa, a lot of that is because our customers went into Africa. We have to provide banking services to our customers going into Africa. That is why much of the time when we go into a market, we go with corporate and investment banking first, just to follow the clients and achieve some cost benefits. And then eventually when we know more about the market, we put a local team in place.'

This business model shows that the private sector is taking heed of the call to contribute towards the development of the continent. Given the bank's stature as a leading bank in South Africa, as well as its slogan, 'Taking Africa to the world', it is financing clients on major projects that are driving development and growth on the continent.

Busi commented that:

'So this is a huge, massive project, but then they would have, I think there is an opportunity to sell them multiple products because we have 2,000 contractors working on a project. It's also an opportunity to sell these people retail banking accounts and you have expats coming in or engineers. Then salaries, offshore, selling products. Then it's around selling them life insurance and healthcare across the value chain – across retail. Possibilities around banking open up opportunities to sell them multiple products and services. And effectively if you take that as an example, both the connection from Africa to China and can also run cross-sell opportunities across retail and wealth.'

As per Todeva[65], 'companies need to become proactive in developing mutually symbiotic relationships with customers, suppliers, and even competitors'. Trusting relationships are built over time and maintaining such relationships and exporting them across borders is a reflection of how these relationships are nurtured. In strong, trusting relationships, high-value clients tend to attract other high-value clients. In this way, social capital is exportable and translated into economic benefit for both parties. How this is applicable is that with Africa becoming increasingly connected through technology and the promotion of intra-regional trade, if a company has a strong brand at home, it is easier to attract new customers in other countries.

> **QUESTION 4: How do you enter these new markets (partnership, acquisition, greenfield, etc)?**

Although the respondents from Sanlam described broadly how the company expands operations into other markets, it was clear that the organisation enters into partnerships with local players *(Table 8)*. The partnership model is preferred as the companies can complement one another, which can mitigate any disadvantages that one company might have. The respondents did note, however, that a partnership needs to be profitable sooner rather than later. In contrast, Standard Bank's approach is to make acquisitions or greenfield investments, i.e., having a majority stake. The ownership model fits well for Standard Bank with its clear motive of dominating Africa and having developed deep internationalisation capability over a century. Companies that are willing to be the first movers in such daunting circumstances can reap the benefits if they use experiential learnings.[66]

Table 8: Business models used to enter new markets

SANLAM: RESPONSES	
Local partner understands the local market	39%
Partnership to complement each other	22%
Internationalisation core competencies	16%
If majority, more power to make decisions	14%
Partnerships profitable sooner	9%

STANDARD BANK: RESPONSES	
Acquisitions or greenfields	39%
Majority stake preferred	33%
Acquisitions reduce lead time to market	28%

CHOICE OF BUSINESS ENTRY MODE

Based on the survey results, the predominant model used by South African companies in their expansion strategies is the joint venture model, and to a very small extent, ownership. The early starters took the first mover advantage and positioned their brands in the market. Matthew articulated how brand and having the right staff go hand in hand:

> 'And then when you have good people, you now need to build the brand – what we stand for, who are we. And a lot of times, this is logical, if any one of these does not fall in place like synchronised, you have a problem. Because even if I have good people and I don't have the brand, they don't build the brand and promote it and make it visible, you don't get to the outcome you want. The fifth point there is to attract the customers if you continue in that line of thought – remember we are a new bank, we have managed to get acceptance and

we managed to find good people; we managed to build our brand, we managed to attract customers, now we can actually decide which kind of customers we want.'

Generally, multinationals do not prefer a sole venture when contractual and investment risks seem high, but the capacity to deal with investment risks depends on their ownership advantages. They may enter markets that are perceived to have high contractual risks using sole ventures when they have advanced their ability to develop differentiated products, they have distinctive capabilities and they have clear motives.[67] The ownership model fits well with Standard Bank, which has a clear intention to dominate Africa and has developed deep internationalisation capabilities over a century. Significant managerial and financial resources are key drivers for the long-term success of any foreign investment.

> **QUESTION 5: Once you have entered the market, what steps do you take to implement your strategy?**

When considering local settings, the participants emphasised that South Africa, despite being an African country that might be expected to have close psychic distances to other African countries, differs as a result of its years of economic isolation under apartheid. In addition, the diverse colonial pasts of African countries led to the use of different languages – English, French, Portuguese, Arabic and others. This is compounded by an extensive range of diverse African cultures.

The participants pointed to the importance of not just localising the business, but also of putting local management in place and ensuring that any solutions are relevant to the local market *(Table 9)*. For Sanlam, there is more reliance on local partners for strategy implementation, so buy-in and commitment to implementation decisions are a high priority. On the other hand, Standard Bank uses the ownership model and follows clients into new markets; it uses client analytics to create integrated solutions for superior client service, using its country-created and experience-based resources.[68]

Table 9: Steps taken to implement strategies

SANLAM: RESPONSES	
Parent company provides expertise	59%
Integrated approach to implementation	22%
Incentives drive behaviour	13%
Effort to speak partner's language bears fruit	3%

STANDARD BANK: RESPONSES	
Integrated approach to implementation	87%
Parent company provides expertise	8%
Parent company staff learning local language	5%

INTEGRATION APPROACH TO IMPLEMENTATION

When the participants were asked how they implement their strategy once a decision has been made, they emphasised that implementation is carried out systematically. Viewpoints that were highly correlated between the two organisations were that the 'Parent company provides expertise' and they have an 'Integrated approach to implementation'. To ensure an integrated approach to implementation, the companies set up special internal departments to work as buffers between the parent and its subsidiaries. The integration teams ensure that, despite the customisation of the business model by a subsidiary, there is a clear understanding of the emerging business model that is finally adopted. These teams are considered essential to ensuring that the policies and the companies' methods of operating are implemented in the destination company.

As Ibrahim said:

'There is pre, during and post type analysis that happens with all the businesses we take on. So, do we look at an acquisition or do we start from scratch? Again, once you are in there, you start running the business and the business falls under SA as we have a team – myself and six of us in the team – who look after everything outside SA on content. There is quite a tight process we follow in terms of integration. We try to bring back business to head office as much as we can to leverage efficiencies. So, our admin and ops are done in SA, with some processing done in-country.'

QUESTION 6: What realities did you face in the destination country during implementation?

The participants indicated that psychic distance creates market conditions that are unique to each of the markets they have operations in.

As Sanlam's strategy is focused on providing insurance for entry level clients, the respondents acknowledged that their entry level clients in neighbouring countries are similar, arguing that entering neighbouring countries is easier for the organisation because of the commonalities. However, Standard Bank, which has been in these markets for longer, believes that it is not just neighbouring countries, but most of their clients on the continent, that are entry level. Standard Bank also sees Nigeria, the largest market in terms of population (220m vs. South Africa's 60m), as a significant market; Nigeria was the largest contributor of revenue and profit to its 'Rest of Africa' division for the 2017 financial year.

Table 10: Realities companies face in destination countries during implementation

SANLAM: RESPONSES		STANDARD BANK: RESPONSES	
Insurance is a luxury	31%	Each market has own local settings	32%
Entry level clients in neighbouring countries are similar	21%	Most markets have entry level clients	32%
South africa is more developed as a market	19%	Significance of nigeria	16%
Each market has own local settings	15%	Cultural differences	11%
Regulatory environment	13%	Regulatory environment	9%

EACH MARKET HAS OWN LOCAL SETTINGS

There was a great deal of commentary on the uneven institutional landscapes in the different geographies due to their cultural differences and regulations. The results, which were corroborated by the survey findings, indicate that the diverse colonial pasts of African countries created a variety of local nuances such as the use of different business languages. This is compounded by an extensive range of African languages and cultures. Africa as a continent is complex and each country has its own unique local settings.

Despite the factors of psychic distance affecting business decisions, African governments are pushing for the localisation of businesses to ensure knowledge transfer and the development of local economies. Most African countries expect localisation for international companies that set up operations; compliance is expected during the tendering process and those that do not have local partners are marked down. The results of this research show indicators of how companies are finding ways to comply with the regulatory landscape and compete in host countries by having local leadership that understands local cultures and norms. Both case companies appoint locals into top leadership positions to bridge the knowledge differences and experiences in the host countries.

> *"I think that each country is different. So it would be arrogant to think that because you have been in Africa for 15 years, when you go to market it will be the same. Localisation is very important. And you should look at our financials as well; some markets we have not really cracked. Why? You look at it, there is a very big difference in culture. There are different language barriers. There is a difference in regulation. Some markets are far more regulated than others."*

In markets with high psychic distance but a good business opportunity, multinationals take steps to bridge the distance by hiring someone with prior knowledge, or someone with country-specific knowledge, who can moderate the effects of the difference.

> **QUESTION 7:** How do you align and customise your strategy and solutions with the dynamics in the destination country?

The results show that both organisations acknowledge the importance of localisation, as the number of responses were almost even *(Table 11)*. The participants pointed out the importance of not just localising the business, but also of putting local management in charge of running the business and ensuring that the solutions are relevant for the market.

Table 11: How companies customise their strategies in a host country

SANLAM: RESPONSES		STANDARD BANK: RESPONSES	
Stakeholder buy-in and commitment	25%	Integrated client solutions	32%
Takes longer to implement	20%	Local management in charge of running business	22%
Local management in charge of running business	20%	Local talent	18%
Local management makes decisions on brand to be used	17%	Localisation important for market acceptance	14%
Localisation important for market acceptance	17%	Client analytics	14%

For Sanlam's partnership model, stakeholder buy-in is very important, however the low risk business entry mode can sustain a long-term view to make it work. The Uppsala Model describes this phased development as an incremental, risk-averse and reluctant adjustment to changes in a company to minimise internationalisation risk. On the other hand, as Standard Bank uses the ownership model and follows clients, it uses client analytics to create integrated solutions for superior client service using its country-created and experience-based resources.

Sanlam relies more on local partners for strategy implementation, so buy-in and commitment to implementation decisions are a high priority. For Standard Bank, because of its extensive experience and time spent in African markets, the focus is on growing the share of the client's business using its competitive intelligence and knowledge management capability for strategic decisions, as well as providing value-added services.

IMPLEMENTATION TAKES LONGER THAN PLANNING

One thing all businesses should be aware of is that implementation takes longer than planning. Sanlam, as a latecomer, mentioned the long period needed for implementation, which was also confirmed in the earlier survey results. What was apparent from the interviewees was that, as planning is done at the head office, it is based on methodologies used for the home business without taking the host country's psychic distance into account. The reasons given were that the heterogeneous landscape and huge cultural differences from South Africa make it difficult to navigate and quickly arrive at a formula that works. For an insurance company, reputation is core to the business model and profitability, and unfortunately, this takes time to build in new markets. Heidi stated:

> 'What we found is that it takes very long. Insurance is specialised, so it takes quite a long take-off. It takes anything from four to six years to actually become profitable. And that is quite a long time, especially in these markets where you really have to create a market. People don't know insurance; you have to educate them.'

She added:

> 'Be patient. In Africa, if you've got to be there, you want to be there for the long haul. We are very confident about the long-term and very confident about our partners.'

According to Matthew's experience:

> 'So obviously there is a process that we follow. So once we have a partner and we start getting into the early deal stage,

we obviously do quite a comprehensive scan of what is out there. You only uncover so much in the due diligence process. So we kind of chunked it up in terms of our engagement model. So in the engagement model we say:

1. *In the due diligence process you have identified things that need attention; whether they will become the conditions that sit in the sale agreement that need to be addressed.*
2. *That then gets followed by a very deep engagement with the country management and the board.*
3. *And then there is a bucket of things, if you will. That from a Sanlam perspective, we say, given our contribution, these are the list of things we want you to do.*

So those are the three areas and the process we typically follow. Now if you ask me whether this covers all our bases – absolutely not. Those skeletons are there. They come out of the closet when you least want them to. If there is collusion between management, there is no way that due diligence will pick up on those things. And those things come to bite you and it becomes very costly. You have your warranties in there but always find it difficult to enforce. So it's fine having it in a legal document, but when it comes to when you have to enforce it, it becomes a lot more challenging.'

My experience working on the continent has pointed to extensive due diligence done by companies considering acquisitions that even involve checking the individual members of boards, just to make sure that there are no obvious things that may play themselves out in the public domain.

QUESTION 8: With the cultural distance between South Africa and destination countries, how do you ensure that the parent company values are consistent in the countries you operate in?

When assessing how the two multinationals ensure there is alignment between the parent and its cross-border subsidiaries, both companies indicated that they ensure that they 'Align behaviours and brand' and use their company-specific advantages of internalised knowledge to manage projects *(Table 12)*. The other common consideration between the two companies is a 'Robust risk management and governance framework'.

Table 12: How companies align the values of the subsidiary to the parent

SANLAM: RESPONSES		STANDARD BANK: RESPONSES	
Align behaviours with brand	26%	Robust risk management and governance	40%
Local partner with similar values	23%	Align behaviours with brand	25%
Brand consistency is managed by parent company	20%	Expatriates	21%
Robust governance	18%	Familiarity with brand	18%
Strong brand used	17%		

For Sanlam, having a partner with similar values is paramount to ensure that there is strategic alignment; whichever company has a stronger brand, that brand is used. On the contrary, Standard Bank's ownership model means that clients have to be familiar with the parent brand, so the alignment of the home and host brands is very important.

EXPATRIATES AND LEADERSHIP WITH INTERNATIONAL EXPERIENCE

The results showed that entering emerging markets is about timing and mode of entry. This means that once the parent company has identified a market, there is a time lag between finding the right local people and running the business. Once located, local managers need training on parent company norms and methods of doing business before they take charge. To ensure that there is no delay in setting up the subsidiary and that the behaviours of the subsidiary are aligned with the parent company, managers from the parent company with international experience are deployed to set up and open the business. These expatriates usually instil and embed the parent company's values, while upskilling local management to fully run the business after a defined period.

Matthew stated:

'So, at the beginning, we need to bridge that skills transfer gap. Even if we find good people in Ethiopia right away, we still need to bring them up to speed with Standard Bank's way of running a business; of doing things. And ultimately, over time, we can reduce the number of expatriates going from here and make sure that key positions and the business are run by capable locals in the country.'

Although developing countries want skilled people to train local professionals, they are strict on the number of expats allowed per company, which limits skills transfers.

Busi explained:

'They want their transformation development programmes to hire locals. They are clamping down on ease and ability to issue work permits.'

Companies must thus have a clear strategy on how they will attract and retain skilled local people to run their businesses. The main mitigation strategy used by Standard Bank is to appoint people from the host countries who grew up in South Africa.

Anne stated:

'You will be surprised to see how many Ethiopians, for example, work in South Africa. We use employment agencies and our own human capital network. The diaspora is a big part of our operations in Africa. I was not born in South Africa, I was born in Nigeria, so if I choose now to go and work in Nigeria, I know the culture, the language. I can go there and work there permanently instead of engaging with them like I do now. So, when they go there, it becomes a perfect fit.'

Although South African labour law expects corporates to adhere strictly to regulations like employing previously disadvantaged local South Africans into senior positions to address the imbalances of the past, a flexible HR strategy that accommodates the complexities of foreign conditions is needed. These include employing African members of diasporas as host country managers, which is likely to boost their internationalisation capability.[69] Expatriates from other African countries who grew up in South Africa and are employed in these South African companies are familiar with the company's culture and are thus better able to bridge cultural and language divides. This also reduces the time needed to upskill local leadership, reducing the transient implementation period. Success comes from having a continental view of human resource management. Such companies see the value in having a pool of continental experts who can easily be posted to a country to set up and run a business.

PARTNERS WITH SIMILAR VALUES

Successful partnerships are built on trust, so it is vital to find local partners who not only have similar values to those of the parent company, but are also familiar with the local legislation and market conditions.

Andre stated:

'When we select our co-shareholders, our partners, we select businesspeople. We don't select people who are politically connected or something, because that's where you get remarks like, "We can't fire him because he is this guy's brother's cousin". But if you choose a partner who wants to make money and is a businessperson and if the business is not making profit, then it's easy for them to agree with you.'

Executives need to be clear about what they look for in a partner, particularly when it comes to values and the way of operating. Investing time in a prospective market and the executive team of a potential acquisition yields results. Not just anyone can lead such a mission; a value-creating, mature individual with a solid understanding of the parent company's way of doing things, who is consciously aware of people's cultures and how they relate to things, is the best selection to champion the search for a partner in a host country. This is not, however, a linear process. Other measures include doing due diligence on all the board members of the potential partner company, as well as inviting executives or senior managers to spend time at the company's head office. There they can engage and familiarise themselves with each other to ensure the right match. The old saying is true: 'You don't know someone until you have broken bread with them'.

3.2 CASE STUDIES OF INTERNATIONALISING COMPANIES

QUESTION 9: What has contributed to your success so far?

After reviewing the state of operations post-implementation, respondents from both companies confirmed that, although greenfields have no skeletons, they take longer to become profitable *(Table 13)*. There was acknowledgement that the African context is not homogenous, specifically when it comes to regulations, culture and infrastructure. For this reason, the success factors of such initiatives have to be viewed differently, and more time should be generally allowed beyond the set delivery deadlines. This is because of the harsh and uneven market places on the continent, which are largely influenced by culture.

Table 13: What contributes to company success

SANLAM: RESPONSES		STANDARD BANK: RESPONSES	
Be humble	26%	Local culture	44%
Diligent implementation	22%	Be humble	34%
Greenfields take time to be profitable	22%	Greenfield long lead time to market	9%
Greenfields have no skeletons	15%	Acquisitions have skeletons	6%
Track record with mixed results	15%	Greenfields do not have skeletons	6%

Both companies currently use the acquisition model for softer landings in new markets. Standard Bank, however, highlighted the risk of acquisitions as often having skeletons, typically related to due diligence. Despite such awareness, there are cases where organisations have failed in their chosen markets. A myriad of reasons for such failures relate to 'copy and paste' approaches, regulatory challenges and sudden changes in market conditions.

As Busi elaborated:

'So, you've got to understand the political culture. You've got to understand your customers. You've got to understand your staff. You have got to take time. Just start with the culture. Because if you miss that you are going to go with the most brilliant ideas and fail and never understand why. And sometimes Africa won't be open to you. You know that passive resistance – things won't just happen.'

Christiaan felt that it is all about having a trusted partner and having aligned goals:

'I can't tell you; it could be five months or six months, some of them took more than two years to put together. You must take your time. You must have discussions. We always bring our partners here first to come and see our business; to understand our operation so that they are not dealing with one person that goes in-country. We bring them here, we take them for a day or two to various departments, to various areas for them to talk to everybody, to get a feel of what our culture is.

'We would have been in their organisation and had meetings with various people to get a feel for their culture. That means you need to have people who understand the organisation to do those investment decisions, to go out to the country.'

> **QUESTION 10: With the cultural distance between South Africa and destination countries, how do you ensure that parent company values are consistent in the countries you operate in?**

Jarred declared:
'If you think of the bank's values, they are almost global. Values are a small thing; I think culture plays a major role. And I think the way we manage it is that you are working towards a specific objective around strategy. From a cultural perspective, there are values and there are the behaviours we expect. But it is not to go and impose our values and our culture per se. You cannot compare a Nigerian bank with a South African bank or a Kenyan bank to a South African one. So, you have a culture in the country that sort of reflects how they do things. You work within the culture of the country but then around the values of the bank.'

Leon elaborated:
'We currently go and engage the countries. We run workshops with staff and it is around saying, "Look, what is the role of values; what are your company values; and how do your values, brand and behaviours work together"?

'And then we take them through a process and say, "These are your values, these are Sanlam's values". They may be using different wording so we will kind of join the dots. And then, I think more importantly, we can look at where Sanlam says, "We serve with pride and integrity". You may have it in your values worded slightly differently but it means the same thing. We want the same thing. But most importantly, the behaviours that we define in the business must give life to those values.'

> **QUESTION 11: What has contributed to your success so far?**

Matthew said:
'I think the first step is that we do our homework upfront – whether it's acquisition or greenfields. Commercially it stakes up rather than just following a strategy blindly. And then implementation plays a big part. We have a team that drives the integration of businesses from start to finish, and I think that helps in ensuring the successful integration and management of those businesses.'

Kabanga noted:
'What I can say is, what works is you get the right local partner, the right local management, you want the right guys on the ground. So you need the right local partner. The right management on the ground and then decent support from centre and maybe a dose of luck. Also, remember that some markets are better than others. I would say that with a good partner, good local management combined with the right people, you should do well.'

> **QUESTION 12: Are there markets you have failed in?**

One of the greatest teachers on the continent is learning from those who have gone before you. Through the feedback and experiences of other corporations and businesspeople, it is not that easy, but it is possible, to piece together what one can expect when exploring the continent. These lessons can enable one to put together a strategy in order to avoid experiencing the same failures as previous companies. The value of these business lessons is that you do not need to experience all of them first-hand.

Anne noted:

'I think it also goes back to how those economies are performing. The countries that are not doing well are largely driven by the size of those economies. So a country like Lesotho, Eswatini, to have a presence there and Zimbabwe even, you are not going to make money in those markets because they are small economies for corporate and investment banking.

'I think a lot of it is driven by risk appetite. So for us to expect to be managing risk, where we want to have the risk and of course what basis. It's making the right choices between the transactions we do, in the capital we hold. For example, in the DRC, we hold large market capital depending on what those returns are. I think from a corporate and investment banking perspective, it's understanding what cap size. But that risk appetite is obviously going to be driven by the size of banks in-country. If you have four banks in a small country, it's difficult for you to make money. But then the opposite is also true. If you have small bank in a big country, you are missing out on the market opportunity. And the other is being a big bank in a small country; I would say in those situations, let's look at Uganda. Stanbic Uganda is the largest company listed in Uganda, but it has a small market.'

Andre stated:

'I don't think we have necessarily failed, but if you ask the question differently and say, have you lived up to or met all the business case assumptions you had when you went to the

market? We have fallen short in some countries, but that is more a factor of time and setting realistic expectations as opposed to failure. I think if someone wants to come from Europe into the continent and they are expecting quick wins, I think they set themselves up for failure.'

> **QUESTION 13: If you were to advise another CEO wanting to enter some of the markets your organisation has a presence in, what would you say? Reflections post-implementation?**

Ibrahim contributed that:
'I think you need to be clear in what you want to achieve. You need to do due diligence around the country. Understand the country issues, cultural issues, people issues. Ease of actually doing business in those countries. I think just an element of perseverance. I do not think there is any one way – I don't think there have been many corporates that have been successful in Africa. The ones that come to mind are probably MTN, Standard Bank and SAB [South African Breweries] being the most successful in Africa. And we hear of other stories of other companies like Tiger Brands being burned in Nigeria. I think it is going into a country with eyes wide open, but also take a long-term view.'

Christiaan elaborated:
'These are the things that they don't teach you in business school, right? I think maybe a few things would be helpful:
a) Try not to go at it alone.
b) Do your homework. But I think do not do your homework from your desk. You start from the desk then catch a plane and go immerse yourself in the market.

c) Go meet people who understand the culture.
d) Understand expectations. We joke here about Ugandan time, for example. They will never ever pitch up for a meeting at a time that has been agreed upon and is set in everyone's diaries.
e) Understand what you are letting yourself in for.
f) So, you have done the research and the numbers all make sense:
   i. The markets are there.
   ii. Get on the plane.
   iii. Go and meet the people.
   iv. Immerse yourself in the country.
g) Make sure that you would prefer a partnership model.
h) When you get on a plane at OR Tambo, go with your technical knowledge and pack loads of patience. Leave the arrogance behind.

Matthew, with his wealth of experience in the internationalisation journey at Standard Bank, was spot on with his insights:
- *The first is that Africa is not a country. It sounds a small point to make but it is one of the biggest points because there is just so much ignorance about the continent and the nuances that come from the different regions and the different countries and how much people hate their countries being misunderstood or being run as one. So that is a huge, huge issue. And I think if somebody doesn't understand that, they start on the wrong footing. And you know that even with neighbouring countries, you cannot refer, for example, to Lesotho as Eswatini or vice versa – you need to know the country and refer to it accordingly. Similarly, someone from Uganda does*

not want always to be compared to Kenya, as much as someone from South Africa does not want to be compared to Zimbabwe. So all those nuances are important.
- *The second one is respect. I can't overemphasise the importance of respecting the countries; the cultures, the laws, their traditions and their ways of doing things are very, very important. Humility matters on the continent.*
- *The third piece of advice is to suspend judgement! Given previous experiences, there is fear among locals in terms of what the foreign companies' motivation is when they enter their countries and what they bring. If you go with an open mind and willingness to learn, that will really give people a good sense of who you are and what you are about.*
- *The fourth one is to find the right people. Really, really, really, find the right people. Whatever it takes, make sure you've got the right people!*
- *The fifth one I would say, is do not underestimate local competitors. They are amazingly good. In all these years, I have really faced some of the fiercest competitors. Some of the best people we have in the business, we got from our competitors because we couldn't bank them.*
- *The second-to-last one – be very clear about your ethical standards upfront. You'll find that the vast majority of Africans have the same ethical stance. So if you are in a country, you can't judge its ethical standards on the basis of the president and his friends and then say Country A is corrupt. The average, confident African is a God-fearing, hard-working person in business. What's also amazing is how advanced many people are on the continent at a professional level because many of them*

studied at some of the best schools in the world. They have travelled extensively and they have worked for very good and reputable companies. Sometimes we come with our narrow minds from South Africa and talk to a guy who has already worked at Barclays, at Standard & Chartered and who spent 15 years in London; he has family in Canada and all of that and you talk to them and all you know is Johannesburg. So sometimes a bit of that understanding helps.

- *And then the very last one is really wanting to be there. People can sense it. If you don't want to be there and you are just there because it's a job or because you have to visit. You will do all the South African things. You bitch about the airport, you bitch about the queues, you bitch about the roads, you bitch about everything, but you will miss out. I always say that Africa's growth is hidden in plain sight and the opportunities are also hidden in plain sight. It's only those who are willing to look who will succeed.*

3.2.5 SUMMARY OF RESULTS: COMPARING THE TWO COMPANIES

Despite both companies being in the financial sector, the two multinationals exhibit stark differences in their characteristics, planning and implementation processes during internationalisation, as shown in *Table 14*.

Table 14: Summary of the case study companies' internationalisation planning processes

FACTORS	SANLAM	STANDARD BANK
PSYCHIC DISTANCE	• Started in neighbouring countries. • Then English-speaking countries. • Then French-speaking countries.	• Started in neighbouring countries. • Then growth markets. • Then english-speaking countries.
COMPANY RESOURCES	• Invest time in host country to acquire local knowledge. • Patience. Learning from doing small deals, taking a long-term view. • Market analysis.	• Business case. • Due diligence. • Economic indicators. • Internal research department.
STRATEGIC CHOICE	• Partnership to mitigate risk. • Local partner that understands local market. • Partnerships profitable sooner.	• Acquisitions or greenfields. • Majority stake preferred. • Follow clients into countries.

The main considerations influencing the implementation processes during internationalisation are listed in *Table 15*.

Table 15: Summary of the case study companies' internationalisation implementation processes

FACTORS	SANLAM	STANDARD BANK
PSYCHIC DISTANCE	• Each market has own local settings. • Regulatory environment. • Entry level clients in neighbouring countries are similar	• Each market has own local settings. • Regulatory environment. • Rest of africa mostly entry-level. • Significance of nigeria.
COMPANY RESOURCES	• Provides resources. • Coordination and integration. • Localisation for market acceptance. • Partner management runs the business. • Patience – taking a long-term view.	• Provides resources. • Coordination and integration. • Localisation for market acceptance. • Client analytics. • Develop integrated client solutions. • Local management runs the business. • Expatriates or diaspora members posted to implement business strategy.
STRATEGIC CHOICE	• Local partner with similar values. • Partner makes decisions on brand to be used – stronger brand used. • Robust risk management and governance.	• Parent in charge of brand consistency. • Use expatriates and diaspora members. • Robust risk management and governance.

Despite Sanlam having a strong brand given its dominant market size on the continent, it does not necessarily trade under its own name in many markets, as most of the decision-making is left for the local partner to make. The partnership structures are set up in such a way that they co-create solutions based on local needs and customise them for the host countries through these partnerships. As a latecomer to internationalisation, its chosen mode of entry is partnering, with a low level of ownership. The robustness of the model lies in finding partners with similar values, who are entrusted with running the business and making management decisions, including the choice of brand to be used in the host market. Despite being a latecomer, this approach has given Sanlam access to 35 countries. This exceeds Standard Bank's reach in terms of number of markets, as it has only targeted 20 countries. For Standard Bank, rapid expansion took place in the initial wave of internationalisation (in the early 1900s), when the bank had a UK-based partner as a major shareholder. At that time, the company's internationalisation was aimed at targeting former British colonies.

3.2.6 HOW DID THESE COMPANIES CONQUER AFRICA?

Companies using the Uppsala Model initially expand to psychically close locations and, after accumulating experiential knowledge, expand further to psychically distant locations. Although both companies use a staged approach, starting with geographically, culturally and institutionally similar neighbouring countries, their internationalisation patterns are different.

For Sanlam, with its experience of doing business in 35 countries, the two themes deemed most important were 'Taking a long-term view' and 'Having a partner with similar values'. Thereafter, it was significant to assess the 'Business opportunity'

3.2 CASE STUDIES OF INTERNATIONALISING COMPANIES

and 'Set targets and track them'. It became evident from the research that, although it is still early in its internationalisation process, the company has consistently managed to grow its footprint on the continent by learning from each subsidiary it has acquired. It does so by effectively managing risk and consciously acquiring minority shareholdings to minimise the impact of failure. The company selectively looks for local partners with similar values for easier alignment. Its approach is to not rush into a partnership, but to allow time to learn about one another's way of doing things to ensure that the two businesses are comfortable working together.

Standard Bank has navigated the continent for over a century, however the results indicate that the organisation is now placing more effort into ensuring that the business model in the chosen markets focuses less on planning and more on implementing and discovering. The bank uses its observed and experiential knowledge of the African landscape to pursue its dominance, offering banking and non-banking services solutions on the continent. To realise this strategy, the company pursues majority shareholding during acquisitions. At times it takes a greenfield approach in markets where there are opportunities but nothing to buy. The strategy is modelled on growth markets, such as Nigeria, Kenya, Ghana and Côte D'Ivoire, where it has seen greater success. The respondents indicated that, although the original entry into the rest of Africa was associated with transactional services, Standard Bank has adjusted over time to where it now uses client analytics and targets high-value clients, offering not only banking solutions, but also non-banking services. This has come about through collaboration within the different divisions of the business and as subsidiaries. Client retention is embedded in its value chains.

Executives and analysts typically search for and analyse data to make assumptions that will be used to inform a decision. It is, however, not how much data you have, but the quality of sources used to obtain that information. By understanding why your customers are your customers in the new market, you can truly revolutionise the types of products you offer them, gain insight into the type of locals you should hire, and understand the types of decisions that will get you over the hill.

3.2 CASE STUDIES OF INTERNATIONALISING COMPANIES

> *"You have got to take time. Just start with the culture. Because if you miss that you are going to go with the most brilliant ideas and fail and never understand why."*

FOUR

WHAT WORKS IN AFRICA

Albert Einstein once said, 'If you can't explain it simply, you don't understand it well enough'. This section aims to provide a practical toolkit as an evolving guide to help corporates in their planning and implementation processes to expand beyond their national borders onto the African continent.

4.1 SUCCESSFUL EXPANSION OF BUSINESSES INTO MULTIPLE AFRICAN COUNTRIES

The research shows that psychic distance, firm resources and strategic choice influence multinationals' planning and implementation processes differently. The two companies in question, a bank and an insurer, expanded using the cyclic management process, where a host of strategic considerations are dealt with in a stepwise planning phase based on the internationalisation motive, leading to a cyclic implementation phase characterised by alignment and customisation of the strategy. This is consistent with previous research, which shows that the internationalisation of banks and insurance companies follows largely similar patterns, where they use their dynamic capabilities to upgrade and reconstruct their core capabilities in response to the changing environment.

4.1 SUCCESSFUL EXPANSION OF BUSINESSES INTO MULTIPLE AFRICAN COUNTRIES

4.1.1 THE TOOLKIT

The cyclic adaptive management process, which is based on the results of this study, indicates that companies expanding operations across sub-Saharan Africa that succeed have dynamic capabilities that develop over time. These companies are always on the lookout for familiarities and differences, and then innovate.

Figure 21: The cyclic adaptive management process from planning to post-implementation

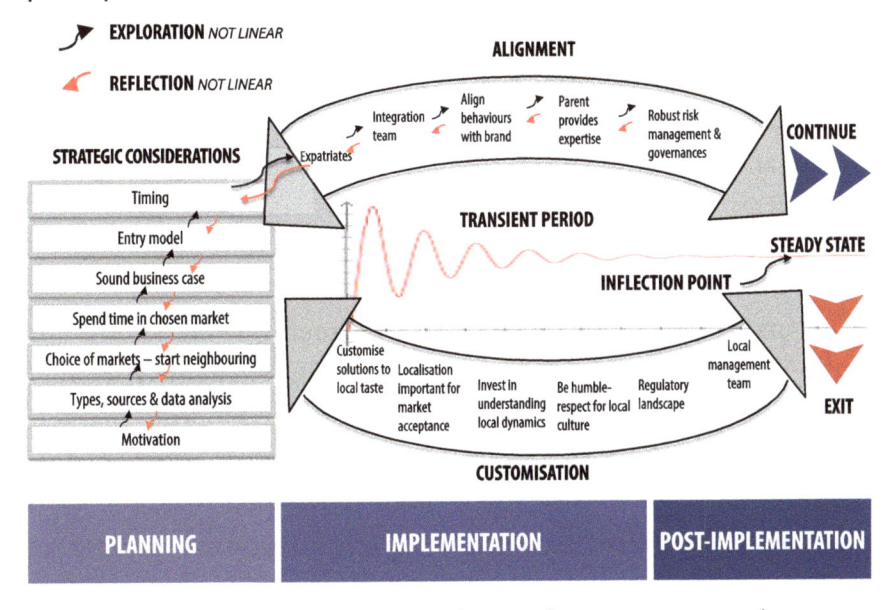

Regardless of the company, a host of strategic considerations can be dealt with in a staged manner.

STRATEGIC CONSIDERATIONS

Given the time it takes to plan and implement internationalisation, companies typically go through iterative planning and implementation processes. Planning should begin with a clear motive and data gathering, using a myriad of internal and external sources to assess market potential. To reduce the risk of 'outsidership', companies must bridge their knowledge gap by sending representatives to the relevant countries to gather tacit market and institutional information.

ALIGNMENT

Using internalised knowledge and capabilities, companies should prioritise the alignment of a subsidiary to the parent company. This is vital to facilitate the alignment of business processes, values and the 'way of doing things' between subsidiaries and the home company. Expatriates with international experience, or even members of a diaspora, can also be used as forerunners to set up and influence the culture until a skilled local management team is appointed.

CUSTOMISATION

The institutional landscape in most emerging markets is not fully developed and, in some cases, is non-existent. Although South Africa has both developed and developing markets, its institutional landscape, in comparison with other African markets, is most similar to those of developed markets. With each African market having a unique institutional and market milieu, local management must be put into leadership positions and empowered to make decisions and run the business. These decisions do not typically follow a linear process.

THE ADAPTIVE MANAGEMENT CYCLE DURING IMPLEMENTATION

The basis of this toolkit highlights a cycle in which strategic considerations give rise to implementation and alignment, which further give rise to customisation. To succeed, a business ultimately needs to incorporate feedback into its strategic considerations. Why is this toolkit necessary? It's about being agile on a continent of consistent uncertainty and challenges. Developing strategies that have room for change is essential to overcome the inherent uncertainty and ensure appropriate responses in the changing African landscape. This cycle is a structured, iterative process of robust decision-making in the face of uncertainty.

Figure 22: The adaptive cycle

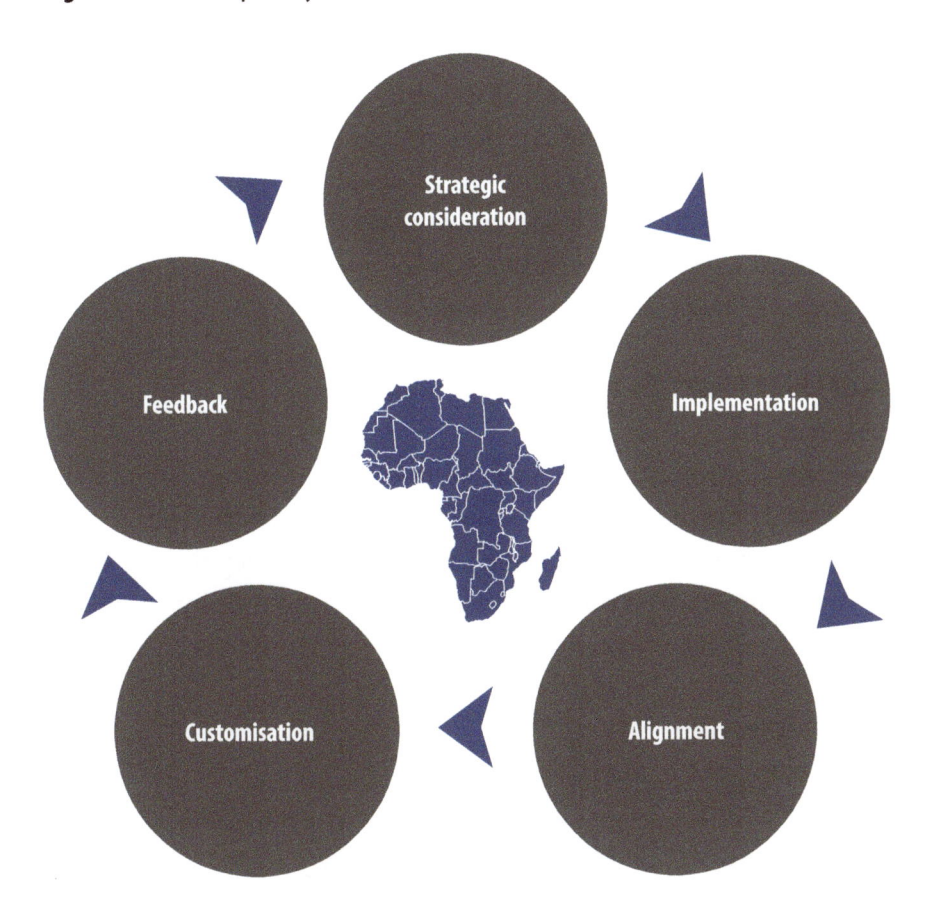

4.1.2 THE PROCESSES
PLANNING PROCESSES

We know that a planning process involves the strategic considerations that companies use for entry into new markets outside their national borders. The key nuances are *motivation, taking a long-term view* and *entry model*.

One of the managers in M&A highlighted the importance of spending time in the target country:

'Attitude is everything we have discussed in terms of respecting people in their country. Respect the culture, respect the regulations and take time to understand how things work in that country, and when you hit the ground, you will be able to render financial services in an environment you are accepted in and where your brand is respected. Much of that has to do with attitude... But oftentimes, these soft points are crucial. Get information and get information from credible sources, not just from anyone, and then have the right attitude.

IMPLEMENTATION PROCESSES
Alignment
During alignment, companies follow similar iterations to those followed during strategic considerations, where the process oscillates between exploration and reflection. Depending on the conditions on the ground, the process gets to a point where the company decides to either scale up or exit the market.

Customisation
An Executive Head stated:

'The advice is to go out there with your eyes open, your ears open and just listen, hear and learn. Be patient.'

Drivers of the transient period

The transient period describes a time when several of the implementation variables are changing. The transient periods for both the ownership and partnership models are affected by a myriad of issues. One of the executives advised:

'Acquire knowledge before you define your strategy; before you understand your blueprint. Know what's negotiable. Know what's not negotiable. And then be realistic; things take a little bit longer in the rest of Africa because of infrastructure, the processes, the governance and many other things.'

POST-IMPLEMENTATION PROCESSES

All possible scenarios for executives considering pursuing new markets should be considered. Exit strategies are as important as entry strategies for corporates; if an exit is not done properly, reputations can be damaged. Although the initial motivation is to explore new business opportunities, contributing towards the economic growth of the continent should be paramount to a company's strategy and long-term approach. Withdrawing from such markets could lead to reputational risk as the host governments may see them as a profit-making, rather than a development entity. Given the expectation that corporates will make a difference in the markets they choose to operate in, there is pressure for these organisations to stay put and to try and succeed.

4.2 LIVED EXPERIENCES FROM LOCALS AND MY PERSONAL EXPERIENCE

Life is a continuous chain of experiences. The time I have spent in many African countries doing business has been extremely worthwhile and nothing can replace lived experiences with theory. My trips and experiential learnings from different countries I have been to, as per *Figure 23* below, are invaluable.

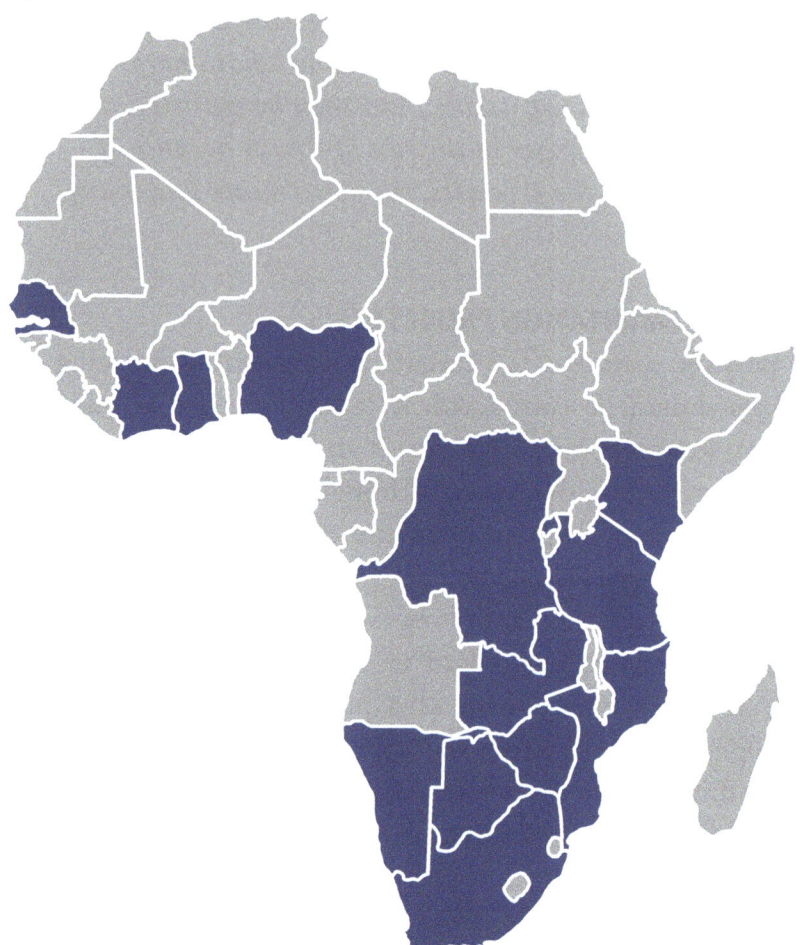

Figure 23: Countries I have done business in

My experiences have provided me with experiential learnings, as well as memories of, and insights from, other Africans, which have enabled me to learn about the everyday realities of ordinary and business life in these different countries. Most importantly, it has equipped me with the soft skills I need to succeed in my clients' chosen destinations.

4.2.1 EASE OF DOING BUSINESS

When companies contemplate doing business in other countries, one of the areas they consider is how easy it is to do business in that country. The more difficult the country is when doing business, the more costly it is to set up and run the business. The attractiveness of a country is thus, to a large extent, measured by how easy it is to do business there.

The World Bank index, *Ease of Doing Business*, is an aggregate that measures and combines different factors that define the ease of doing business in a country. Countries are ranked against each other based on this global index, which broadly focuses on regulations for businesses and protection of property rights. The 10 parameters of doing business from which the information is collected include:
- starting a business;
- dealing with construction permits;
- access to electricity;
- registering property;
- getting credit;
- protecting minority investors;
- paying taxes;
- trading across borders;
- enforcing contracts; and
- resolving insolvency.

Each of the above metrics are scored at a country level – the higher the ranking on the *Ease of Doing Business*, the better the country's business environment.

According to the most recent *Ease of Doing Business* rankings from 2021, New Zealand was the easiest country to do business in, with a Doing Business (DB) score of 86.8, followed by Singapore with a DB score of 86.2. In Africa, Mauritius and Rwanda were the only two sub-Saharan African economies in the Global Top 50, with DB scores of 81.5 and 76.5 respectively. In the total list of 190 countries that were ranked, Libya (186), Eritrea (189) and Somalia (190) were the lowest ranked economies in the region, with DB scores of 32.7, 21.6 and 20.0 respectively. Sub-Saharan Africa remains one of lowest ranked regions with an average DB score of 51.8, well below the global average of 63.[70] *Table 16* below shows the African Top 10 with their respective DB scores.

Table 16: Africa's top 10 countries for Ease of Doing Business[71]

TOP 10 COUNTRIES IN AFRICA	AFRICA TOP 10	GLOBAL RANKING	DOING BUSINESS SCORE
MAURITIUS	1	13	81.5
RWANDA	2	38	76.5
MOROCCO	3	53	73.4
KENYA	4	56	73.2
TUNISIA	5	78	68.7
SOUTH AFRICA	6	84	67.0
ZAMBIA	7	85	66.9
BOTSWANA	8	87	66.2
TOGO	9	97	62.3
SEYCHELLES	10	100	61.7%

4.2 LIVED EXPERIENCES FROM LOCALS AND MY PERSONAL EXPERIENCE

Below I discuss some of the countries that I have spent time doing business in. In Africa, business innovation, creativity and entrepreneurship comprise the backbone of most economies. To foreign companies that enter some of these markets, certain companies succeed, while others battle to find the winning formula.

To get a good understanding of how locals feel about the business environment and what entering such markets and setting up businesses would mean for foreign companies, I interviewed some business people in selected countries on their view of doing business in their respective countries. To draw out nuances, the individuals were asked the following questions:

1. In your view, what do foreign companies struggle with when they set up business in your country or anywhere in Africa?
2. What would your advice be to these companies?

4.2.2 RWANDA

Rwanda is ranked 2nd in Africa for ease of doing business, after Mauritius.

Given that most African governments require foreign companies to pay fees (~US$1 million) to set up business in their countries, this can be a huge deterrent, especially for businesses from Africa. Rwanda is changing the narrative, however, by creating investment incentives for people to set up businesses, given that they will contribute towards the development of the country. I travel to Rwanda regularly and have begun exploring registering my business there. Fortunately I have had some reassuring conversations with government agencies such as Rwanda Finance and the Rwanda Development Board, which have assured me that my business will be registered within six hours from filing the required documents. Planting and operating a business in Rwanda is straightforward; your company simply needs to:
- create quality jobs;
- transfer skills and technology; and
- innovate.

My overall experience has been that the government is very deliberate in making locals feel a sense of ownership. The country has set a long-term vision and created shared values between the government and communities. The spirit is about, 'What can I do for my country?' What has been quite poignant is having national activities that bring communities together such as Umuganda, which takes place once a month and sees residents 'come together in common purpose to achieve an outcome' by doing community work in their neighbourhoods. The government has also made certain activities cheaper for locals, such as audio tours at the Genocide Memorial and tickets for the Visit Rwanda bus, to ensure that they can experience their country and be ambassadors for it. It is no surprise, then, that Rwanda is positioning itself as the jewel of Africa.

4.2 LIVED EXPERIENCES FROM LOCALS AND MY PERSONAL EXPERIENCE

'As the government is encouraging sustainability, safety and foreign business start-ups, for outsiders to register their businesses and get an investment certificate, the company needs to demonstrate that they will create quality jobs, they will transfer skills and will have innovation and creativity at the centre. My business has been in operation for the past 15 years and to expand I will need a cash injection. I am glad that some foreign private equity companies are looking at investing in my company, which will help the company grow. That availability of foreign capital has made Rwanda attractive to other African countries.'
Jacob Ingabire, Entrepreneur, Rwanda

4.2.3 ZAMBIA

Zambia is ranked 7th in Africa for ease of doing business.

During the 1980s, Zambia was struggling economically and imported most of its basic goods from Zimbabwe. Eventually, the country became less reliant on imports and focused on being business ready, positioning itself to be a trade centre. This was relatively easy as the country shares a border with eight other African countries. As a Zambian once explained to me:

'Given that each of the African countries got their independence at different times, Zambia has become accustomed to harbouring people fleeing unrest in their different countries. Zambia is, therefore, a cocktail of many different cultures. The country has proven itself to be a very welcoming place, with people keen to learn from those coming from the outside. Zambia is one of the friendliest places in the world to live, do business, work and play. Its rich cultural and religious diversity has made it a home for people of various ethnic backgrounds and lifestyles.
If one is humble enough to learn, the locals are open to assisting you to grow'.

Other Zambians shared their thoughts:

'I suggest that all investors planning to export goods from our country to the rest of the world should probably import their own equipment into Zambia to help process their materials into refined goods. The investors coming to Zambia should be cautioned to improve corporate social responsibility to uplift certain developments in rural areas, such as power generation, water reticulation, telecommunications, street lightings, and road construction.'
Vincent C. Nguvulu, Founder of Beyond Foundation Zambia, Speaker and Author of Beyond University, Zambia

4.2 LIVED EXPERIENCES FROM LOCALS AND MY PERSONAL EXPERIENCE

'Vodafone Zambia launched its operations in 2016 and as it emerged, it got many consumers of its products with the release of a 4G Wi-Fi router. Not many of us in Zambia knew how fascinating this was. We were all excited to try out the new adventure of fast internet browsing without a need of buying weekly bundles from our local network operators in Zambia. In the attempt to penetrate our local markets, Vodafone Zambia offered life-changing experiences to its participating customers.'
Wanzi David Lungu, Creative Director and Web Designer at Canvasigns, Zambia

4.2.4 GHANA
Ghana is ranked 17th in Africa for ease of doing business.

Ghanaians believe in getting things right and emphasise finding solutions through innovation. Many businesspeople who began as entrepreneurs end up with a portfolio of businesses. I remember one executive of a large bank saying that he listens carefully when his clients speak about their businesses, their needs and their challenges, and this is what has inspired his other businesses. This kind of thinking inspires the way I now do things, and I have started motivating my children to have a portfolio of things they can do. This advice inspired me to start my own consulting company.

'Foreign companies struggle with understanding the different procedures relating to the minimum capital requirement for trading companies, sole proprietors and JVs. This is a huge deterrent for many businesses, as some might not have sufficient capital. Another thing is how to navigate regulations and ensure full compliance. A possible way to succeed would be access to the right people, channels, and business networks.'

Bruce Yaw Addo, Director of Africa Trade and Investment Council (NPC), South Africa & Managing Partner at Infusion Africa, Ghana

4.2.5 NIGERIA

Nigeria is ranked 21st in Africa for ease of doing business.

In Nigeria, regulations are not always clear and one needs to deal with local intermediaries to understand them. On top of that, changes in market conditions can occur very quickly and market structures are ambiguous. This means that one needs to spend time on the ground to have a good understanding of the nuances. For example, Nigerians are used to doing business in difficult environments, such as:

4.2 LIVED EXPERIENCES FROM LOCALS AND MY PERSONAL EXPERIENCE

- loadshedding more than 50% of the time;
- deteriorating road infrastructure; and
- low regulatory clarity.

What I enjoy about Nigeria is that Nigerians are very competitive. During my induction into Nigeria one of my colleagues said to me, 'Please excuse us when we speak to each other; we speak very loud'. When I asked why, she replied, 'Because in Nigeria we are too many. We learnt at an early age to speak loud so that we can be heard. Remember we are competing with many other people for attention'. For me, this explained why Nigerians are generally very competitive and have an abundance of confidence. So, for an outsider, it is very important to gain a good understanding of the issues under discussion. You would not want to embarrass yourself by not being prepared and seeming as though you are not adding value. As a confident people, Nigerians can 'sell ice to an Eskimo'; they will market a product or service that is still in its infancy phase and figure out the nuances of the business model as they go along.

One experience I still cherish was attending the local wedding of my associate. My host colleagues made me traditional attire, organised shoes and other accessories, and ensured that I felt like a princess. This was necessary as I was attending an access card-only wedding. In many African countries, especially in rural areas and townships, guests usually arrive through word-of-mouth advertising, rather than through an invitation. That entire experience taught me that Nigerians love the glitz and glamour, and value work relationships. Above all, the best way to understand the local environment is to experience local norms and cultures with them.

'Formalisation of business documentation is a challenge, and these regulations change regularly. So new companies need to be sure they understand what the law is before they even start doing business. It's the same with understanding the tax terrain. Another challenge is infrastructure inefficiencies, such as electricity and general support structures from government. This means that the company should be adaptable. Finally, cultural adaptation is essential for success, but Nigerians are not particularly difficult people to get along with.'
Otobore Olumoye, Principal Partner at Tobore Olumoye Consulting, Nigeria

'Foreign companies may struggle with the task of finding competent staff, the poor state of infrastructure, a lack of market information and data, red tape, bureaucracy and erratic government policies, the high cost of business financing, lack of trust from the market. Also a highly

volatile exchange rate, security (insurgency, terrorism, and kidnapping), political instability and even a hostile business environment that could worsen ease of doing business. These struggles are exhaustive, depending on the sector. To cope with a hostile business environment, businesses should have a proper understanding of the sector they operate in and the taxes and levies to be paid. To address the issue of infrastructure, business should be sited close to sources of raw materials due to poor road infrastructure. Also, businesses can explore renewable energy sources, such as solar energy and an inverter. It could be capital intensive initially but will pay off later after subsequent use. Staff of these companies must understand the various policies of the government and significance of compliance so as not to run afoul of the law, which would heighten operational costs. In terms of security, locations where the insurgency rate remain worrisome should be avoided.'

Waheed Alimi, MBA, FCA, ACTI, ACIS, Managing Partner at KEWIG Consulting, Nigeria

4.2.6 TANZANIA

Tanzania is ranked 25th in Africa for ease of doing business.

My first experience of Tanzania was in June 2021, at the height of Covid-19. Tanzania was one of the few countries that did not impose any lockdown, but had other ways of trying to keep Covid at bay. After we had landed, everyone did a rapid Covid-19 test. If it was positive, you were quarantined. If not, then it was business as usual. Business in Tanzania is very relational. As in many other African countries, foreigners are typically allocated a full-time driver and food is ordered at most high-level business meetings. Tourism is usually something your colleagues want to experience with you to ensure that you experience the best of Tanzania – especially their international tourist attraction of Zanzibar. For those who love the bush, the Serengeti, with its iconic 'great migration', is a must do. My experience in Tanzania was warm and reinforced that they are caring people with a level of hospitality that is the best I have ever experienced on the continent. During my short stay, I was taken to experience local cuisines, experienced very respectful office cultures and was given gifts to share with my business partners back home.

From a business perspective, my experience in Tanzania points to finding a partner where there is mutual interest. Once you find one, your partner will hold your hand and welcome you into their family. This level of openness allows goals to be achieved at a faster rate; my executive team went out of their way to make me feel comfortable.

> *'Most foreign companies struggle during registration of their companies in Tanzania. They face a lot of bureaucracy and corruption incidences. They also have a challenge of acquiring working permits for their employees. I think Rwanda has done well in solving these two issues. My advice – let the foreign companies work first with a local partner to study the system and then create valuable networks in government offices. After that, the other processes will be smoother.'*
> **Rodrick Nabe, Public Speaker, Corporate Trainer and Author, Tanzania**

4.2.7 DEMOCRATIC REPUBLIC OF CONGO (DRC)

The DRC is ranked 48th in Africa for ease of doing business.

The DRC is the largest country in central Africa in terms of land area. Widely considered to be the richest country in Africa due to its natural resources, these are also believed to be the reason for war being endemic to the country. Doing business in the DRC is, therefore, very difficult because of its limited infrastructure. When I was exploring opportunities in the country, given that the main official language is French and I am English-speaking, it also quickly became clear to me that one needs a local intermediary to explore opportunities. The language barrier is one reason why having agents/facilitators is common, yet using agents can create a challenge in terms of the legitimacy of a business transaction, as some rely largely on who they know. My key learning in the DRC has been that for a new business venture to work, you need to consider partnerships. That is, unless you are prepared to invest in spending time in the country to understand the market dynamics, what the real opportunities are and how to realistically translate these opportunities into a profitable business.

'I believe many foreign companies would love to launch their business in Congo but there are so many challenges. For example, the level of corruption in the country regarding bribes and paperwork can result in problems like fraudulent licenses and paperwork. Another thing to consider is that companies will not be able to sell their products to people that don't have jobs and don't receive salaries.'
Ben Kamba, Entrepreneur, DRC

4.2 LIVED EXPERIENCES FROM LOCALS AND MY PERSONAL EXPERIENCE

'1. I believe many foreign companies will love to install their business in Congo but there are so many challenges. For example, when the country is full of corruption the companies will have problems because everyone want money in his pocket to make things easy and shortcut for the companies to get paperwork and stuff. Unfortunately, later on they will have problems as the initial documents were not the right papers or licenses as the "officials" who issued those initial papers were not the right people.
2. Some companies will struggle because of lack of infrastructure such as electricity, water and roads.
3. The poverty may also be another BIG problem. Companies won't be able to sell their products to communities they operate in as most of them do not have jobs and hence do not receive salaries.'
Fortunat Kamba, CEO of Total Diamond International & Founder of The Longindo Foundation, DRC

FIVE

FINAL INSIGHTS

Dr Elizabeth Nkumbula (Founder and Chairperson of ENVIS Consulting Limited; Board Chairperson of Zambia International Trade Fair Trust; Commissioner and CEO of the Workers Compensation Fund Control Board in Zambia from 2012 to 2019) was generous enough to share some invaluable insights with me on doing business in Africa.

> **QUESTION 1: In your view, what do foreign companies struggle with when they set up business in Zambia or anywhere in Africa?**

a) **Finding skilled labour and skilled talent** is a major challenge for companies setting up business in Africa. Yet while the skills gap in the labour market is still very high, Africa has a young, highly educated and eager population, that when given the right training and guidance, are capable of exceeding at any task or job that they are assigned.

Many companies that have been successful in Africa have recognised that they can gain a competitive advantage by focusing on meeting the labour demands and skills requirements of their industry/sector by offering on-the-job training and support to their employees.

Some businesses are also actively seeking to adapt and improve their existing internal knowledge base by establishing programmes to share skills and experience across generations. For smaller businesses in Africa, an approach could be to encourage and support staff in gaining skills that the company sees a demand for in the near future. For example, skill sets like data analytics and programming can be encouraged amongst staff who have the potential and are willing to learn. In a nutshell, businesses both large and small must begin to reconsider their talent acquisition and development strategy.

b) A widespread lack of access to electricity in Africa is another major challenge for businesses. Africa's access to electricity significantly lags compared to the world, and there are significant regional and country variations in terms of access to electricity within the continent. This insufficient supply of electricity can significantly increase the operational costs of businesses, which sometimes have to develop self-sufficient solutions to stay operational.

In the coming years, it will be critical to harness other sources of energy, such as solar and biofuels, to supply businesses with the fundamental infrastructure they require, rather than creating a typical electric grid, particularly in remote areas. Businesses should begin to think about renewable energy alternatives and look at how they can be funded individually or collectively.

c) Supply chain challenges mean that moving around in Africa can be a logistical challenge. Poor infrastructure and the multiple challenges involved in moving between countries are a major cause of disruption in a business' supply chain. Not only can it be difficult to get goods efficiently to the end customer, but it can also be challenging for people to meet up to facilitate business transactions in a region where face-to-face meetings are prioritised in order to build trust.

Because transportation is a major barrier in many African countries, manufacturers have to devise creative ways to transport their goods. For instance, Coca-Cola in Africa has a small army of entrepreneurs who take over where trucking ends by walking or biking products the last mile to their delivery destination. It is thus important for businesses to find innovative approaches to the distribution challenges that they face, and partner with local service providers.

d) Difficult regulatory landscapes and ever-changing government policies remain a problem; even through African countries have shown significant progress in improving their ease of doing business, more can be done to make Africa even more competitive on the global stage. Across the continent, it can be quite challenging to start a business, enforce contracts, register new property, get regulatory permits and protect investors.

It can also be difficult for businesses to build consistent long-term plans, which inherently increases the cost of doing business in Africa. Businesses need to come together and become more strategic and proactive in their dealings with government by being unified in discussing their challenges, as that will enable policy makers to create policies that consider the needs of the private sector.

e) The high cost of securing capital means that bank loans often come with high interest rates due to the perceived risks of doing business in Africa. With the advent of Fintech, businesses in Africa are now able to access financing at a more equitable rate, and with less onerous terms and conditions placed on them.

> **QUESTION 2: What would your advice be to these companies?**

Considering the increasing affluence, population growth, urbanisation rates and rapid spread of access to the internet and mobile phones on the continent, Africa's burgeoning economies present exciting opportunities for expansion in a range of sectors. However, the African business landscape can present unique challenges that are not often encountered outside of the continent and can make it challenging doing business in Africa.

To successfully access Africa's significant economic opportunities, businesses must establish creative business models and robust strategies that are specific to their target markets. Companies must be aware of the potential challenges and issues so that they can factor them into their business models whilst developing their innovative initiatives. However, obstacles will vary among the continent's 54 countries.

To make progress in this area, these challenges must be overcome if Africa is to achieve its growth goals in the next decade. Businesses that innovate to assist individuals and other businesses in overcoming these challenges will achieve huge success in Africa. What the continent can do for itself to create and capitalise on the commercial prospects it provides is to continue to invest in infrastructure; thus far, investment levels are on pace, despite infrastructure lag.

To create more jobs, many African countries must focus on supporting the formation of large and medium-sized businesses. To do this, education systems that are currently geared to producing civil employees must be modified. Schooling should incorporate more career and technical education skills, and nurture entrepreneurial ideals.

On a final note, multinational corporations must respond to Africa's actual reality. Doing business in Africa is unlike doing business anywhere else. You are unlikely to succeed if you approach the situation from a European or American perspective. Opportunities exist if you can adapt and have a patient strategy.

In conclusion, despite the challenges facing the African continent, trade and investment opportunities continue to thrive. The future of Africa looks bright with continued investment in technology and progressive policy initiatives, such as the African Continental Free Trade Area (AfCFTA).

5 FINAL INSIGHTS

"*To successfully access Africa's significant economic opportunities, businesses must establish creative business models and robust strategies that are specific to their target markets.*"

SIX

CONCLUSION

Africa is larger than the United States, China, India, Japan and the whole of Europe put together, yet there is a misconception that the continent is like one homogenous country, rather than 54 unique nations, each with its own regulatory landscape, traditions and cultures. Although some cultures and languages span across countries, historical contexts and political landscapes, amongst others, create unique local nuances for each country. The clear cultural differences mean that in-person relationships are important to build trust. As it takes longer to cultivate such relationships, a dose of patience and localisation is needed to cultivate trust and show that you are in it for the long haul and there to participate in the economic growth of the communities you decide to serve. Doing business in Africa requires a long-term view, but once you develop trust, it is easy to grow your network. In summary, despite the African challenges that usually loom large, in those challenges, there lie the opportunities.

Some of the key challenges include:
- insufficient market data;
- difficulty finding the right talent;
- an everchanging regulatory landscape;

6 CONCLUSION

- poor infrastructure (roads, electricity, etc.); and
- local cultural nuances.

Multinationals looking to succeed and contribute towards the economic development of the continent must respond to Africa's realities. With its large population growth, natural resources and growth in the number of people who have access to the internet, there are a myriad of business opportunities, yet the strategy companies use to explore business in Africa matters.

My experiential learning has shown that multinationals face intense competition from local competitors in African markets, which is why they have to craft bespoke strategies for expansion outside their national borders. The case studies confirmed the findings of previous studies, i.e., that banks and insurance companies follow largely similar internationalisation patterns. The case studies also highlighted complexities such as the need for local legitimacy, the tacitness of local cultures and protracted implementation periods that cannot be explained by traditional foreign direct investment theories. Companies develop non-market resources by spending periods of time in a potential host country before setting up operations, so that they can gather information and build hands-on market intelligence based on experiential knowledge of the local market.

Standard Bank, whose first wave of internationalisation, as with other major banks, was in the late 1800s, uses the ownership entry mode. While literature has shown that companies acquire local partners when there are high psychic distances, because bank services require a high degree of information, information transfer and trust[72], risk management is very important. Good governance and ethical leadership are key for success. This case study revealed that because bank values such as integrity and accountability are global, a subsidiary's aptitude to demonstrate its ability to work within a country's culture while retaining the values of the bank earns respect from regulators and customers, and increases market share. It is also clear that to bridge psychic distances in the initial stages of internationalisation, some companies use expatriates with global experience, and in certain cases, they use diasporas from target countries. A number of these companies build a pool of skilled African diaspora, who are citizens of the host market, to manage and facilitate the integration process and bridge the cultural gap, thereby shortening the transient period.

While literature has shown that banks and insurance companies follow similar internationalisation patterns[73], when a business enters a certain market determines its entry mode. First movers, because of the knowledge they acquire over time, can afford to use the ownership mode, whilst partnerships tend to appeal to latecomers, although they require a lot of work to identify the right partner. Learning from "small deals" in different geographies is a low risk strategy to understand how business is done in the different markets. In addition, leaders who believe in spending time in different markets to understand local nuances acquire insights that help them adapt strategies to local nuances and customer tastes.

Regardless of whether an ownership-based or a partnership-based model is used, distance and cultural integration are important determinants for both internationalisation strategies. Although the case studies of Sanlam and Standard Bank revealed similar internationalisation patterns, such as starting in psychically close locations, using financial resources to fund the protracted implementation of the strategy and having local management run the business in the host country, the companies differ greatly on the entry mode, timing of entry and decision-making process. As it is very difficult to leave after making a massive financial investment in a market, most companies tend to put a lot of effort into trying to make it work, until they get signals to either scale up or exit with minimal reputational damage.

What is quite apparent is that among African countries, there are cultural similarities and also some glaring differences, which are influenced by the ease of doing business, economic factors, regulatory landscape, etc. When I started my journey, I could not fathom riding on a motorbike as a 'taxi', as all I had seen were bikers who were a law unto themselves. However, countries such as Rwanda ensure compliance with traffic rules, and in those countries, I am now very comfortable using a motorbike as a mode of transport.

Culture, the level of entrepreneurship and infrastructure development can be quite different between countries. Local nuances such as language, regulatory landscape, natural resources, etc., create unique settings that require insight to navigate. Having an understanding of these different local dynamics and being able to find the sweet spot for your business is key.

Spending time in different countries has given me a great appreciation of my continent. I have met many people from different walks of life and heard numerous inspiring stories from businesspeople about how they got started. In many cases, what is now a flourishing business simply started with a need to survive or a dream for a better life.

> A story I love to share is the story of a businessman I met at an event we hosted when I was based in Ghana. His entrepreneurial journey started after school, when he joined other cross-border entrepreneurs selling goods in

neighbouring Benin as there were no job opportunities back home. On his way back to Ghana he would bring goods from Benin to sell locally. After doing this for a while, he decided to set up a shop in Kumasi, the business hub of Ghana, as he felt comfortable that he had a large enough client base. He soon realised, however, that the shop that he thought he had acquired exclusive rights to sell his goods in was also leased to three other tenants. He spent months fighting to be recognised as the rightful tenant through the court. But as the case dragged on and he watched his financial resources being depleted, he had a light bulb moment… If four people had to share a lease to one property, it was a sign that there was huge demand for commercial property in Kumasi. He immediately pivoted his business to commercial property. When I met him in 2018, this entrepreneur was a dollar millionaire who owned a huge commercial and residential property business. He also imported luxury cars from Canada and hair products from China, and had a local loan business. This is a typical example of a fearless entrepreneur in Africa who sees opportunities to solve problems on the continent.

I have learnt that, as human beings, we are multi-talented and multi-skilled and should not let opportunities pass us by; it is important to consider multiple projects to hedge our risks. The power of social networks can also not be underestimated. The chances are high that for whatever we want or need, there is someone in our network who knows someone who can help; it is all about nurturing and using our networks to grow and expand our reach.

6 CONCLUSION

My life has led me to understand that experiential knowledge is empowering. Despite foreign companies having massive resources, competitive capabilities in host countries stem from being able to localise the business to suit market conditions. The alignment of a business model with that of the home country, the customisation of products and services in the destination country, and the localisation of businesses, are fundamental. Harnessing the capabilities of the continent requires leaders who do not back away at the first sign of failure, but who are committed to the economic development of the continent while growing their company's bottom line. Successful leaders can work within a country's culture while following the values of the company, thereby earning respect from regulators and customers alike. These leaders need to invest time and effort in understanding how business is done the 'local way', by identifying and selecting partners with similar values and goals, as well as by adopting a learning culture.

To many outsiders, Africa is one big continent where cultures, norms and traditions are similar. The reality is, however, that Africa, with its 54 countries and varying domestic institutions, as well as multi-ethnic, multi-language, multi-religious and diverse colonial histories, is not a 'one-size-fits-all' landscape. Doing business in Africa is easier for those who are good listeners and observers; people who are keen to learn. The more one embraces and has an appreciation for the continent and its rich cultural diversity, the more one can build a sustainable business that is embraced by locals. Opportunities abound in Africa – from a young and growing population to a narrowing infrastructure gap and a penchant for innovation. ***Carpe diem!***

SEVEN

REFERENCES

[1] Chen, C., & Orr, R. J. (2009). Chinese contractors in Africa: Home government support, coordination mechanisms and market entry strategies. *Journal of Construction Engineering Management*, 135(11), 1201-1210.

[2] Matano, S. (2020). Indian companies in Africa leveraging commerce systems, *Mitsui & Co*, Retrieved from: https://www.mitsui.com/mgssi/en/report/detail/__icsFiles/afieldfile/2020/05/22/2003c_matano_e.pdf

[3] Dunning, J. H. (1988). The eclectic paradigm of international production: A restatement and some possible extensions. *Journal of International Business Studies*, 19(1), 1-31.

[4] Jain, N. K., Hausknecht, D. R., & Mukherjee, D. (2013). Location determinants for emerging market firms. *Management Decision*, 51(2), 396-418.

[5] Barney, J. B. (1991). Company resources and sustained competitive advantage. *Journal of Management*, 17(1), 99-120.

[6] Porter, M. E. (1980). *Competitive strategy*. New York, NY: Free Press.

[7] Khanna, T., & Palepu, K. G. (2006). Emerging giants: Building world class companies in developing countries. *Harvard Business Review*, 84(10), 35-46.

[8] Fletcher, R., & Fang, T. (2006). Assessing the impact of culture on relationship creation and network formation in emerging Asian markets. *European Journal of Marketing*, 40(3/4), 430-446.

[9] Pugh, J., & Bourgeois, L. J. (2011). 'Doing' strategy. *Journal of Strategy and Management*, 4(2), 172-1791.

[10] Khanna, T., & Palepu, K. G. (2010). *Winning in emerging markets: A road map for strategy and execution*. Boston: Harvard Business.

[11] Williams, D. W., & Grégoire, D. A. (2014). Seeking commonalities or avoiding differences? Re-conceptualizing distance and its effects on internationalization decisions. *Journal of International Business Studies*, 46(3), 253-284.

[12] Horner, S., Baack, D., & Baack, D. (2016). The role of psychic distance in internationalization strategy evaluations and strategic choices. *Journal of Business Strategies*, 33(1), 17-47.

[13] Williams, D. W., & Grégoire, D. A. (2014). Seeking commonalities or avoiding differences? Re-conceptualizing distance and its effects on internationalization decisions. *Journal of International Business Studies*, 46(3), 253-284.

[14] Johanson, J., & Vahlne, J.-E. (2009). The Uppsala internationalization process model revisited: From liability of foreignness to liability of outsidership. *Journal of International Business Studies*, 40(9), 1411-1431.

15 Perks, K. J., Hogan, S. P., & Shukla, P. (2013). The effect of multi-level factors on MNEs' market entry success in a small emerging market. *Asia Pacific Journal of Marketing and Logistics*, 25(1), 131-143.

16 Institute of Cultural Diplomacy. (2023). *Introduction to the African Diaspora across the World*. Retrieved from: https://www.culturaldiplomacy.org/index.php?en_programs_diaspora#:~:text=The%20word%20%E2%80%9CDiaspora%E2%80%9D%20has%20its,the%20actual%20process%20of%20dispersal.

17 Contractor, F. (2013). 'Punching above their weight': The sources of competitive advantage for emerging market multinationals. *International Journal of Emerging Markets*, 8(4), 304-328.

18 Harvey, M. G., Speier, C., & Novicevic, M. M. (1999). The impact of emerging markets on staffing the global organization: A knowledge-based view. *Journal of International Management*, 5(3), 167-186.

19 Buckley, P. J. (2018). Internalisation theory and outward direct investment by emerging market multinationals. *Management International Review*, 58(2), 195-224.

20 Hoskisson, R. E., Eden, L., Lau, C. M., & Wright, M. (2000). Strategy in emerging economies. *Academy of Management Journal*, 43(3), 249-267.

21 Buckley, P. J. (2018). Internalisation theory and outward direct investment by emerging market multinationals. *Management International Review*, 58(2), 195-224.

[22] Accenture. (2009). *Expansion into Africa: Challenges and success factors revealed*. Cape Town: Accenture.

[23] Cuervo-Cazurra, A. (2008). The multinationalization of developing country MNEs: The case of multinationals. *Journal of International Management*, 14(1), 138–154.

[24] Prahalad, C. K. (2004). *The fortune at the bottom of the pyramid: Eradicating poverty through profits*. Philadelphia, PA: Wharton.

[25] Bhattacharya, A. K., & Michael, D. C. (2008). *How local companies keep multinationals at bay*. Retrieved from: https://hbr.org/2008/03/how-local-companies-keep-multinationals-at-bay.

[26] London, T., & Hart, S. L. (2004). Reinventing strategies for emerging markets: Beyond the transitional model. *Journal of International Business Studies*, 35(5), 350-370.

[27] Munir, N. S., Prasetyo, A., & Kurnia, P. (2011). Garauda Indonesia: To becoming a distinguished airline. *Emerald Emerging Market Case Studies*, 1(1), 1-33.

[28] Bowman, E. H., & Helfat, C. E. (2001). Does corporate strategy matter? *Strategic Management Journal*, 22(1), 1-23.

[29] Sterling, J. (2003). Translating strategy into effective implementation: Dispelling the myths and highlighting what works. *Strategy & Leadership*, 31(3), 27-34.

[30] Eyring, M. J., Johnson, M. W., & Nair, H. (2011). New business models in emerging markets. *Harvard Business Review*, 1(1), 89-95.

[31] Madhok, A. (1997). Cost, value and foreign market entry mode: The transaction and the firm. *Strategic Management Journal*, 18, 39-61.

[32] Dunning, J. H. (1988). The eclectic paradigm of international production: A restatement and some possible extensions. *Journal of International Business Studies*, 19(1), 1-31.

[33] Khanna, T., & Palepu, K. G. (2010). *Winning in emerging markets: A road map for strategy and execution*. Boston: Harvard Business.

[34] Perks, K. J., Hogan, S. P., & Shukla, P. (2013). The effect of multi-level factors on MNEs' market entry success in a small emerging market. *Asia Pacific Journal of Marketing and Logistics*, 25(1), 131-143.

[35] Horner, S., Baack, D., & Baack, D. (2016). The role of psychic distance in internationalization strategy evaluations and strategic choices. *Journal of Business Strategies*, 33(1), 17-47.

[36] Khanna, T., & Palepu, K. G. (2010). *Winning in emerging markets: A road map for strategy and execution*. Boston: Harvard Business.

[37] Williamson, P., & Wan, F. (2018). Emerging market multinationals and the concept of ownership advantages. *International Journal of Emerging Markets*, 567(3), 557.

[38] Hoskisson, R. E., Eden, L., Lau, C. M., & Wright, M. (2000). Strategy in emerging economies. *Academy of Management Journal*, 43(3), 249-267.

[39] Borchardt, W. (2009). *Expansion into Africa: Challenges and success factors revealed*. Cape Town: Accenture.

[40] Boateng, A., Du, M., Wang, Y., & Wang, C. A. M. F. (2017). Explaining the surge in M&A as an entry mode: home country and cultural influences. *International Marketing Review*, 34(1), 87-108.

[41] Sterling, J. (2003). Translating strategy into effective implementation: Dispelling the myths and highlighting what works. *Strategy & Leadership*, 31(3), 27-34.

[42] Khanna, T., & Palepu, K. G. (2005). Strategies that fit emerging markets. *Harvard Business Review*, 83(6), 63-76.

[43] Simon, S. (2009). *Start with why: How Great Leaders Inspire Everyone to Take Action*. London: Penguin Group.

[44] UN Environment Programme. (2022). *Our work in Africa*. Retrieved from: https://www.unep.org/regions/africa/our-work-africa.

[45] The World Bank. (2021). *Ease of doing business rankings*. Retrieved from: https://archive.doingbusiness.org/en/rankings.

[46] World Economic Forum. (2021). *Why foreign direct investment is key to Africa's sustainable recovery*. Retrieved from: https://www.weforum.org/agenda/2021/08/foreign-direct-investment-key-africa-sustainable-recovery/.

[47] Ibid.

[48] Ibid.

[49] Statista Research Department. (2021). *Forecast of the total population of Africa 2020-2050*. Retrieved from: https://www.statista.com/statistics/1224205/forecast-of-the-total-population-of-africa/.

⁵⁰ Khanna, T., & Palepu, K. G. (2006). Emerging giants: Building world class companies in developing countries. *Harvard Business Review*, 84(10), 35-46.

⁵¹ African Business. (2021). *Africa's Top 250 Companies in 2021*. Retrieved from: https://african.business/dossiers/africas-top-companies/.

⁵² Ibid.

⁵³ African Business. (2022). *Africa's top 250 companies*. Retrieved from: https://african.business/2022/05/dossier/africas-top-250-companies-in-2022

⁵⁴ Global Africa Network. (2017). *South African business expands into the rest of Africa*. Retrieved from: https://www.globalafricanetwork.com/2017/12/05/company-news/south-african-business-expands-into-africa/.

⁵⁵ McKinsey & Company. (2020). *Connecting with customers in times of crisis*. Retrieved from: https://www.mckinsey.com/capabilities/growth-marketing-and-sales/our-insights/connecting-with-customers-in-times-of-crisis.

⁵⁶ Govirandajan, V., & Trimble, C. (2011). The CEO's role in business model reinvention. *Harvard Business Review*, 89 (1-2), 108-114.

⁵⁷ Sanlam.(2022). *About Sanlam*. Retrieved from: https://www.sanlam.com/

⁵⁸ Ojewake, C., & Oladipo, O. (2023). Nigeria has Sanlam's fastest growing insurance business in Africa. *Business Day*. Retrieved from: https://businessday.ng/interview/article/nigeria-has-sanlams-fastest-growing-insurance-business-in-africa-werth/.

[59] Standard Bank Group. (2022). *About Standard Bank Group*. Retrieved from: https://www.standardbank.com/sbg/standard-bank-group

[60] Vahlne, J.-E., & Johanson, J. (2013). The Uppsala Model on evolution of the multinational business enterprise: From internalization to coordination of networks. *International Marketing Review*, 30(3), 189-210.

[61] Cuervo-Cazurra, A., & Genc, M. E. (2011). Obligating, pressuring, and supporting dimensions of the environment and the non-market advantages of developing-country multinational companies. *Journal of Management Studies*, 48(2), 441-455.

[62] Horner, S., Baack, D., & Baack, D. (2016). The role of psychic distance in internationalization strategy evaluations and strategic choices. *Journal of Business Strategies*, 33(1), 17-47.

[63] Enderwick, P. (2009a). Large Emerging Markets (LEMs) and international strategy. *International Marketing Review*, 26(1), 7-16.

[64] Enderwick, P. (2009b). Responding to global crisis: The contribution of emerging markets to strategic adaptation. *International Journal of Emerging Markiets*, 4(4), 358-374.

[65] Todeva, E. (2014). Business network theory and the role of country of origin. *Presentation at the XVIII ISA World Congress of Sociology, Facing an unequal world: Challenges for global sociology, July 13-19*. Retrieved from: https://isaconf.confex.com/isaconf/wc2014/webprogram/Paper67029.html.

[66] Hoskisson, R. E., Eden, L., Lau, C. M., & Wright, M. (2000). Strategy in emerging economies. *Academy of Management Journal*, 43(3), 249-267.

[67] Nunes, P., & Breene, T. (2011). Reinvent your business before its too late. *Harvard Business Review*, 89(1/2), 80-87.

[68] Jain, N. K., Hausknecht, D. R., & Mukherjee, D. (2013). Location determinants for emerging market firms. *Management Decision*, 51(2), 396-418.

[69] Harvey, M. G., Speier, C., & Novicevic, M. M. (1999). The impact of emerging markets on staffing the global organization: A knowledge-based view. *Journal of International Management*, 5(3), 167-186.

[70] World Bank. (2020). *Doing Business 2020*. Retrieved from: https://openknowledge.worldbank.org/server/api/core/bitstreams/75ea67f9-4bcb-5766-ada6-6963a992d64c/content

[71] Ibid.

[72] Fischer, S., & Hasselknippe, A. (2017). *The internationalisation of banks: A comparative case study* (Master's thesis). Department of Business Studies, Uppsala University, Sweden. Retrieved from http://uu.diva-portal.org/smash/get/diva2:1116009/FULLTEXT01.pdf.

[73] Focarelli, D., & Pozzolo, A. (2008). Cross-border M&As in the financial sector: Is banking different from insurance? *Journal of Banking and Finance*, 32(1), 15–29.

Milton Keynes UK
Ingram Content Group UK Ltd.
UKHW020643311024
2488UKWH00031B/212